fabrication:

essays on making things and making meaning

by **Susan Neville**

MacMurray & Beck

Printed and bound in the United States of America

1   2   3   4   5   6   7   8   9   10

Library of Congress Cataloging-in-Publication Data
Neville, Susan
Fabrication : essays on making things and making meaning /
by Susan Neville.
p.   cm.
ISBN 1-878448-08-0
1. Manufactures. 2. Technology and civilization. I. Title.
TS146.N48   2001
303.48'3—dc21   00-048195

Fabrication cover design by Tangram Design.
The text was set in Adobe Garamond by Pro Production, Mahwah, N.J.

For May Iske

CONTENTS

Acknowledgments

Thanks to Barb Shoup, Tom and Shirley Brown, Al Tivotta, Virginia Gillette, John Grunewald, Joe Weigel, Malik Hakeem, Fritz Frohmeyer, David Hoppe, Jim Poyser, Aron Aji, Jim Frias, Andy Levy, Michael Martone, Kent Calder, Grace Farrell, Tyagan Miller, Shirley Daniell, the Indiana Historical Society, and Butler University.

Portions of this book have appeared in *Arts Indiana, Black Warrior Review, Evansville Review, Krestrel, Nuvo, Traces of Midwestern History,* and *Twilight in Arcadia (Indiana Historical Society Press).*

Fabrication

I wrote this book in an office in an abandoned automobile factory. I wrote it because one morning I realized I didn't know the difference between the diesel engine of the bus that takes my children to school each morning and the gasoline engine inside my car. I didn't know how the rectangle of art glass that hangs in my kitchen window was made, or the doll on my daughter's shelf, or the gyroscope that spins in my son's hand. I didn't know who made the steel for my car or who designed my mother's coffin. Because I wanted to know how these things were manufactured, and by whom, and how well, and what they meant, I've spent the past two years walking through factories. I've seen how the process of canning tomatoes is similar to the process of making metal caskets. I've watched one woman paint eyelashes on a doll's face while another stabs a row of vinyl babies' heads with an icepick. I've watched blue globes spin through a room exactly like planets and tobacco being grown and auctioned for cigarettes. I've seen a man carve the excess wood off Christ's hipbone, while other Christs wait patiently on an assembly line. And I've seen wrecked cars and sand consumed and then transformed by fire. I was looking, I know now, for something to be awed by. And because I myself am a fabricator, I was drawn to the craft, the processes, the mysteries of fabrication. Essays are structures built of separate pieces the way you build a house out of boards and nails and stone and clay and time. I've learned new words like *flange* and *extrude* and *lathe* and *machine* as a verb, as in *to machine*. And *sprue*. See how the right and left edges of this paragraph are aligned? The perfect right angles formed at the corners of the block of text? I love the fact that *fabrication* means *to make* as well as *to make up,* that *factory* has echoes of both *fact* and *story,* that simple words can be both justified and true.

HOW THE UNIVERSE IS MADE

My next-door neighbor owns seven white dogs. They're all outside this morning, all quiet, all running gracefully through the grass like the ghosts of deer. The dogs are small, rare, well-behaved, and odd-looking breeds. The two largest dogs are whippets, English greyhounds, spooky and muscular. They fly back and forth across the six-foot fence between our houses, and it's utterly soundless, just a smudge of white one way and then the other. Their job is to be mysterious, weird, earthbound angelic birds in the form of dogs. Sometimes they seem like that and sometimes they seem too thin and crouching, sneaky and rabid, all toothy smile.

Every day begins like this for a writer: with the vain attempt to try to get to, in words, something that's just beyond where words stop. This is your job—to throw the rope of words out and try to catch it, then to walk across the rope until the air gets tired of pretending to hold you up and the imaginary rope dissolves and you're plunged into a canyon.

Though sometimes you take a leap across the canyon without a rope at all, a blind leap that doesn't involve faith, just the hope that there will in fact be a way to return to where you started. Either way, you often fall. Then you climb back up the rock face, skin your knees and hands, and throw the rope again. This is your trade, your work, what you do every day of your life.

And so: I still don't have those whippets right, how dreamlike strange they are to me. I could throw words at them for the rest of my life and not quite get at the mystery. I wish that I could be a whippet, an earthbound mammal that gives the illusion of flight. Why do the dogs fly over the fence and back? Maybe they sense something in the air and think they can catch it in their teeth.

What I love in this world is both the whippet and the rope of words.

My neighbors have giant gumball machines and neon-striped jukeboxes and antique rose-colored lamps and antique sinks and a stained-glass fox in the kitchen window and glass green walls. Two weeks ago they built a playhouse by the drainage creek. There are green lawn chairs for the children on the playhouse porch. The chairs are an intense green, not an indigenous color.

My neighbors create their home at every moment, which involves both making things and tearing things down. Last week the husband was up in a sweet gum tree with a chain saw, balancing on a heavy branch, and sawing off the limbs at the tip. Whack! Thud! The screech of the chain saw coming so close to his own powerful leg, and his three children squealing, and the seven white dogs and the wind and the pile of leaves and bark! Whack! Thud! And a gathering of boys around the basketball hoop to play and to watch, and the sun setting all orange and green and shining on the chain saw's metal teeth. And when he got the thing de-limbed it was right through the trunk until the whole tree fell, and then two seconds through the trunk of a dogwood and it was down too, and my neighbor standing there like Paul Bunyan, getting all the kids to carry limbs taller than they were out to the street to be carted away with the next day's trash.

And within two minutes he and his wife decided not to have the stump ground all to hell, as they'd originally planned to do, and instead to build an octagonal bench around it and scoop out the center to grow geraniums.

The whippet's job is to jump, my neighbors' job is to build a life interesting enough to hold seven dogs, two cats, and three children. And my job is to make things up, which has nothing to do, often, with inventing something new. I just sit here patiently picking up each object on the assembly line of perceptions and then picking up the word that goes with that perception and placing it back down on the belt. Whippet. Wind. Paint-green chair on the playhouse porch, that kind of satiny sheen that candy takes on when it cools. Pick up the image. Package it in words. Inspect the sound. Pass it down the line. Next sentence. Next image:

Whippet. Wind. Ghost. Sweet gum tree. The light hits the top branch of the white pine, the metal perch on the bird feeder, the intricate mesh of the porch screen, one white rock. One red-haired neighbor checks the chlorine level in her children's aboveground pool. Two fat red cardinals pick up sunflower kernels and fly to a branch of the black walnut tree.

Those are the things I can see. There are other things I take on faith. At every moment neutrinos pass back and forth through all these things that seem so solid and impenetrable—the bodies of the walnut tree, the cardinals, these fingers—as though we're not even here. The neutrinos are invisible, but apparently have mass. Where are they going? Flying through our bodies and the bodies of whippets and chain saws and boys playing basketball and the insubstantial wind like that. This is the neutrino's work.

Pick up the image. Wrap it up. Lay it back down. Pick up another, do the same, lay it down. Now and then there's one that feels like the canyon's edge, a simple image on an assembly line that opens somehow magically into a vast landscape, and I leap off of or toward it. The difference between a detail and a metaphor. Transubstantiation. You begin with one and end up with both. Sometimes the wine stays wine. Sometimes it's both wine and spirit. You always start with wine. The first miracle.

So drink this down: Inside the white dogs' and my neighbors' bodies and my body and your own, there are, in addition to neutrinos, viruses. The virus's work, it seems, is to get its DNA into the host cell's RNA. According to a new study at Purdue University, the virus does this in the same way you insert a part into a car: by creating its own simple machine. Think about it. The virus makes an octagonal hole in the RNA and shapes the DNA into the same octagon and the whole thing works like a bolt in a pair of human pliers and it looks exactly like the bench my neighbors want to build around the sweet gum's stump.

To say that the universe tends toward disorder seems counterintuitive. Things seem, instead, to tend, through labor, toward further complexity and to follow some sense of aesthetics and shape, some pattern, and it's all more mysterious and awful and lovely than we can even begin to fathom.

In January, scientists announced they had discovered eternity. The universe doesn't have an end, a canyon drop. It keeps expanding. It's at the edge that the universe makes itself up as it goes along. It's here in the center or the edge of center or wherever it is we are that we do the same. So that every cell, every massive and invisible neutrino, every virus, every particle and wave, every boy playing basketball, every neighbor building a playhouse, every whippet flying over a fence, every single living thing that does its work each day helps to make the universe.

ON MAPS AND GLOBES

My daughter spins a globe and asks me questions.

Who put these lines, she asks, across the continents? And how much blood was used to draw them? And who keeps the record of the bridges and the lanes on this connecting road? And who decided on the color of this county?

And what's the distance between here where I'm living out my life, and there, where you live yours?

And if we took the places where we're standing, and we pinned them both together, behind the point where we were joined, would there always be a fold or pleat of shadow?

And if the stars are rushing out toward some edge, is the distance between each molecule increasing?

Of course I tell her I don't know.

And I ask myself about the distance between a real and a made-up place, between this hill and that abstraction, between this word and understanding, between transgression and forgiveness.

I try to find some answers to these questions, but most days the evidence seems inconclusive.

Every day this week a globe has risen orange and tangled itself in the branches of the eastern oak tree. Every day this week the globe has disappeared and left a brief vermilion cloud in the branches of the western sycamore. In between, the blue between the earth and stars was so unseasonably intense it shattered windows. What do I know that I can count on knowing again tomorrow? The sun rises, the sun sets, but from what I can observe it might as well be pulled by chariots. The earth might as well drop off to nothing at the edge right there behind my neighbor's.

I need someone who's been someplace to tell me where I am and how to get to someplace else.

He hovers over a light table, North Carolina spread beneath his fingers. A negative made of something like cellophane, as red as cherry Jell-O, covers the entire table. He moves a jeweler's glass from one place to another. All the other lights are off. Even the shadows in the room are red, and the round lens of his glasses, and the steel of the X-acto blade's reflecting red, and he's cutting and peeling the red plastic negative to get a perfect line.

It's these hands that scribe the microscopic lines that tell you whether the road you want to travel has two or four lanes and where the exits are. He cuts the parallel lines between one highway shoulder and another so cleanly on the red negative that the printer's ink will be trapped between the lines, a good clean fill. If he cuts a jagged line, it will look like hell, and you're liable to think there's a jog in the road ahead, when there isn't one.

He's done this job for his entire working life.

On a good day, the cartographer will focus so completely on the line that the world outside the light table completely disappears or, rather, the world becomes that line and he lets himself fall into it. This is the zen of cartography. If the blade is dull or the red too brittle, or if his concentration slips, he has to begin again at the beginning. If he focuses on the entire project, he says, the trip is overwhelming. If he focuses on the point where the blade meets the negative, time disappears. North Carolina, Australia, Greenland, New York City: it's always the same trip.

And it always begins where someone else left off. Like poetry, a map is an attempt to bring the whole of the physical universe into one point where you can see it, an attempt to bring what seems like chaos into something meaningful on a human scale. We map the ocean, and we map what we see of the stars. The question is always what metaphor to use, what shape to scatter these disparate points across, what shape will most closely resemble the mystery of the thing itself. Like journalism, a modern map is always an attempt at objectivity, yet always somehow subjective, always an attempt to bring wildness under control.

This cartographer alone in this red-lit glowing heart of a room in Indianapolis could easily get us lost. He could confuse us, but he won't. A cartographer draws a line between here and there so that we can find "there" when we want to. The line shows that someone's been there. It shows that we can get there. This room is devoted to accuracy, to being as correct as human beings can be, which is to say that in certain ways we are deluded. Greenland is not that big. The sharper your focus, the more the map has the shape of the land it's abstracting, the more it resembles the thing itself.

And once, the cartographer explains, despite all the edits each map goes through, the company sold a map of the United States for fifteen years before a little girl in Tucson, Arizona, discovered that the name of her city was misspelled. The final edit.

Mapmakers steal whatever they're allowed to. The content comes from the place itself; they can copyright a certain combination of font and color. Now and then a cartographer will insert a mythical place to foil potential plagiarists—a town named after your company, the name of your girlfriend's mother—and the cartographer can choose a color for the land or ocean and you can choose the font, but for the most part you're not allowed to be creative. You don't add flourishes, you don't draw gargoyles in uncharted lands; a modern map doesn't call attention to its fabricated nature.

But it is fabricated. It's an illusion of realism. Someone in Australia called last week and wants to put that continent in North America, and why not? Who says that North is up and South is down? You can't just make a world, you have to think about these things and what they mean.

And then there are the changes in fashion. Wrought iron's a big deal now. Everything used to be mahogany, then along came distressed maple. Colors begin to look like last season's colors, the continents wearing old-fashioned, worn-out clothes.

So how is the world made?

It's made in two hemispheres, and in the shape of a flower.

Each hemisphere is drawn with twelve petals. The ocean is the color of the sky, the lettering is black, and the continents are shades of green and orange and purple. The rosettes are broken in odd places. A tip of New South Wales floats with New Zealand. Half of Zimbabwe floats with Angola and half with Madagascar. The Galapagos Islands are cut in two and there's an entire blue petal with nothing but the South Atlantic Ocean. Look at your globe closely, and you'll see that it's printed on paper in the shape of orange slices.

The world is made in nine and twelve and sixteen inches. The world is made in blue and antique. The world is made in paper and in plastic. The world is made in standard shades and in colors like kiwi and in inks like cobalt and gold that look expensive for those places that need to be filled with conservative, expensive-looking globes. The world can talk, the world can be flat or bumpy. The world can be lit from without or within.

And here's the painful truth:

The world is made on an assembly line. Every day, hundreds are created.

There are so many of them made. How could each one possibly be special?

And how could there possibly be exploding stars, my daughter asks, and were they ever for one second important in some cosmic scheme, and is our sun really going to burn itself out and when it does, are there other worlds being born somewhere to take our place?

And when they take our place, if they do, what will happen to, among other things, Shakespeare? Will God keep *Romeo and Juliet* up there with His collected works? How will *King Lear* hold up alongside the classics of some backwater near Alpha Centauri or some part of the sky we haven't even mapped yet?

My daughter overhears the teenage siblings of her friends. Oh yes, you are the special one, my only love, dame Juliet, dear Romeo, and without you I couldn't live one more second. All day long I think of you.

Here in the globe factory, there are stacks and stacks of flattened worlds and hundreds of spinning globes suspended from the ceiling. There are hundreds of them all rolling down parallel tracks, all constantly moving from here to there, from one side of the universe of this warehouse to the other until they're folded into boxes.

How was the morning after the big bang? my daughter asks. Did worlds explode like this and was there someone there to hang them up in space exactly where they should go, to find the best possible place for that candle sconce, that chandelier, the proper setting for this whole experiment.

The universe where the worlds are made, I said, smells oddly like a bowling alley.

And how was it formed, this world?
Sexually.
After the rosette is cut, the scrap discarded, it's joined to cardboard and formed into two half shells by machinery that comes, again like flowers, in genders. The female part is a metal mold engraved with mountains. The male part is a pole that pushes the cardboard down into the mold and allows the petals of the earth to come together into a half sphere. When the male and female parts have joined together, the mountains swell up on the earth's surface, and the hemispheres are hot to the touch.

They're so hot it takes a while to cool.

Once they do, they move to the drill press, where they dance and spin with joy, off-center like hula hoops; the rough edges are trimmed, and it begins again, this sexual process, this paper mating. A bead of glue is placed on a diaphragm hoop and inserted partway into one hemisphere and then the other hemisphere slides down onto the cardboard hoop until they're joined finally in marriage, the north and south, the up and down, the yin and yang, and then the balls roll down a track like the tracks where they store bowling balls—that metaphor again.

But even after marriage, there's still a crack, as there is in any human system, and something could insert itself and split the two asunder if it weren't for the woman whose job is to put a thin strip of self-adhesive equator tape around the belly. Globe after globe, she affixes equators, the thinnest tape. There can't be a wrinkle; it has to cover the crack completely and it's a tape the size of a line you'd draw with a felt-tipped marker. She's done this for ten years, eight hours a day. If she makes a mistake, that entire world is ruined.

So she pays attention to each and every one. Some days she tapes two thousand globes on one shift. Thirty-five people work each day in the globe department. The sparrow falls, they see it. The equator woman is good at what she does. She hardly ever makes mistakes.

Of course the plastic worlds are something else entirely. The human skill is entirely in the speed you work and in your ability to stay out of the way of the machinery.

There's one large machine that heats the printed plastic and then a gust of air sucks the plastic down into a hemisphere. Over and over, a woman places the plastic on a machine, the machine sucks, the woman places the plastic, the machine sucks. She takes the plastic hemisphere and places it on a stack of other hemispheres like a stack of helmets. OK, I admit it. I hate plastic. The machine sucks. I love the paper globes.

Remember the part in *West Side Story* where Maria spins before a mirror and sings? The sight of one thousand worlds hanging from the ceiling takes your breath away like good music, it does, but my favorite thing in all of creation is the moment when the globes move one by one, like teenagers, in front of something like three showerheads, three blow-dryers, and they twirl around like Maria while they're covered from head to toe with shining lacquer. They go into this room all preteen dull and they come out sixteen years old with shining hair and singing "I Feel Pretty."

There used to be a man here spraying the top, then the middle, and then the bottom all day long, but now this is one area where the globes are all alone, without the parents, and they dance for joy and come out of the ballroom with glazed and shining secret faces.

And I dearly love the spinning lathes and the dark unglobed room where two men stand and fabricate the metal bases and meridians from coins of blank steel. There's no brilliant color here, but without the base, the world's globes would roll off tables, back behind living room sofas.

On a lathe it only takes five seconds to take a flat coin and spin it into the shape you want. Like the lacquer room, you get this rush somehow from your eye feeling the surface of the metal spin into folds and waves, like the earth's crust. The men hold two poles, in the shape of hedge clippers, their arms out like they're pushing a wheelbarrow, and the lathe spins and they push the metal coins against the chuck and voilà, it's a rounded base. Then they cuff the small edges on another spinning wheel.

Of course the base they're spinning could literally be stamped in some more automated process, but these two men would lose their jobs, and for now the capital investment would be greater than the salaries and benefits paid to them. So this is a process on its eventual way out, unfortunately. Because there's something in the way these men work the lathe, like a potter at the wheel or a weaver spinning yarn, where you can see the shape taking form because of the rapid turning that echoes the way a teacher uses a flashlight and a finished globe to show the spinning of the still unfinished earth. It's a kinetic and at the same time metaphorical knowledge of the way the universe was formed. We felt it long before we knew it, that is, if we know anything at all. The lathe, on the other hand, feels true and sturdy, the way you feel some hand against your shoulder when you wobble too far one way or another.

There's no substitute for this kind of knowledge. You have to feel it.

And why is the world still made like this when all the maps you need are on computer programs? In addition to the globes, there are more than ten thousand maps in stacks against the wall or being rolled and cut on tables. Political maps, physical maps, historical maps: a map of the Colonial Possessions of World Powers in 1914, another of Europe in 1648, still another showing Voyages and Discoveries to 1610, and another of Western Land Claims and the Ordinance of 1787. Why all these anachronistic objects? Why are all these people working? Why the postal service shipping these boxes? Why is all this necessary?

I know the answer to that one, my daughter says. It's because, she says, they're pretty things. And when someone is talking with real children in a class and someone asks where is Romania, the teacher can take minutes to go to the computer and call something up upon the screen or she can pull a map down from the ceiling or send the globe on one more rotation around the classroom, passed hand to hand, right there.

And it only takes a split second. And your hand might brush against your teacher's hand, or your best friend's, or some boy you like. It's the way it is, she says, when you pass those plates of glass cups at church.

I run my hand across a globe. You feel the body of the earth when you do this. You feel the roll of mountains, the smooth surface of plateaus. You feel the ocean. You sense the children who have gone before you. You think of the mysteries of travel and return. You think of gravity. Your body remembers a particular basketball and hoop, a particular car trip to Florida, the love that binds you to one place and not another one. And through that one place, if you love it deeply, to every other place there is, to every possibility.

Everything you need to know, my daughter says, the answer to every single question you could think to ask your teachers. For that one moment, you can sense the answers. For that one moment only, it's right there in your hand.

BYZANTIUM

I've sailed the seas and come . . . to B . . . a small
town fastened to a field in Indiana.

—William Gass,
"In the Heart of the Heart of the Country"

It was a short trip to the casket factory. Much shorter
than it looked on all the maps.

I drove through winter's first spitting sleet to get here
and still arrived two hours early for my appointment.

What should I do? I've already eaten breakfast.
I don't know a soul to call for some companionship. I
didn't expect to wait and haven't brought a book.
I don't feel like writing. I'm sick of coffee. It's election
day, and I've already voted.

I could drive around in circles, but my car feels
close and cramped and particularly cluttered.

Though it wasn't a bad drive. I crossed several rivers
to get here, as you might expect. Clifty Creek and dribs
and drabs of moisture with names like the Muddy Fork

of the Sandy Stream. Now and then a splotch of farm-house. It's the first week in November. I couldn't live here this time of year, in this wet and grayish-yellow putrid fog.

I've voted badly. Every lever I pulled was a half-guess, a coin toss, or a prayer. I'm disgusted with myself, and it's spiraling out all Yeatsian.

I'm the worst writer I've ever known, the worst wife, the worst mother, the most unrepentant child and friend. I never exercise. I never eat vegetables. I never return phone calls. I don't recycle. I'm sick to death of the millennium. My head aches. I have a cold. My hands look sticklike and ancient on the steering wheel.

I need a fresh start. I need a clean slate. I'm willing to make a million resolutions once I think of them. I'm starting my new life right after this visit. I swear I am.

So why was the drive to the casket factory so short? I want to get this over with. What do I do with these extra hours? I seem condemned to be alone here with myself. What's wrong with me? I need people and warmly lit interiors. I need a clean, well-lighted human place, and instead I'm in Batesville, Indiana—Byzantium.

Thank God, there's something open.

It's 7 a.m., and the wood-carvers have been working for hours. They're right across the street from the large factories where they make the caskets and the hospital beds, including those warming cribs for newborn baby children.

The outside of the woodshop is that tacky Pennsylvania Dutch–looking gingerbread, all red and blue and yellow symbols, or at least it seems that way to me this morning. I hate this style. Wooden tulips and oompah bands and lederhosen. Long German words that sound like gargling. Perhaps it's only my continued mood. I go inside because I'm bored and it's the only thing open at this hour. I don't expect much.

Inside, there's a shop filled with stained and polished wood. Maple, walnut, cherry, oak. Seals of the state of Indiana and bentwood rockers. Carousel animals and hand-carved fruit, mantels for your fireplace, gun cabinets with secret compartments, and children's toys. All intricately carved, all carefully made, as though it was worth spending time on, as though it was important.

I recognize this stuff. I've gone to circuses and burned logs in the fireplace and pulled the lever in voting booths. I've inherited glass-front cabinets for curios and dishes. I have young children and elderly relatives. On a morning when I'm not on my way to the casket factory, it feels as though I've always been walking on this earth between dependent generations. It feels as though it will always be this way.

But today it all seems strange. How strange the things we find to fill our time with. How strange our hands are, and our thoughts, and our noses and lungs and circulatory systems. How strange that we fall in love, how strange that we build houses. How strange that we have children. How strange that there are people. How good that we don't all have days like the one I'm having simultaneously, that there are forces working to keep the world dead center in its daily spin.

I couldn't work here every day. There are faces carved in wood all over the walls, and every one of the human beings who wore one of these faces is dead. The faces of presidents and saints and sainted football coaches. Every one of the faces, when it was on a living human being, was carved somehow from the inside out. If only I'd known in middle school that you create your living face. I would have been much happier. But now these faces, all this flesh, is gone, no longer changing, replaced by wood all petrified, and someone has carved them from the outside in. You can stare at one of these faces for the rest of your life and it won't move or think another thought or kiss your forehead.

Clearly, this is not a good day for me to go to the casket factory. I'm not ready. I should have gone, instead, to a movie. I know I shouldn't think like this.

An entire woodshop room is filled with Virgin Marys. An entire room is filled with nativities. An entire room is filled with baptismal fonts. We ship them all over the world, my tour guide says. We ship them to cathedrals and country churches. Sometimes the infant is sprinkled. Sometimes the infant is dipped in oil and water and comes up red and choking, all covered with the glossy oil like blood and mucus. A second birth, a second chance at life. Yes, that's what I need today. Please. I'm a weak and sinful swimmer. I've got an appointment at the casket factory. Hold me under.

In the back of the shop, there are two blond brothers holding chisels. The wood is white and soft, and covered with grooves from the knife blades. The room is like a hospital, and there are tables covered with white and naked corpses.

Like the faces, the corpses are emerging from the wood. Perhaps it isn't from the outside in, as I had thought. It's like they're surfacing, these pale bodies, like the infants through the baptismal water, like some large fish from underneath the ocean, like something oddly invisible rising up through the air, from someplace underneath what you can see.

The wooden corpses range in size from an infant's body to an adult male. One carver is working on a large body. It's Boniface, he tells me. How do you do this? He seems so real. It seems impossible. All these statues lying on the tables.

He shows me a drawing he's made. It's beautiful, like a cemetery rubbing, something medieval. The drawing itself is something you'd spend years on. Most of this I've done, he said, motioning to the saint's body, with a chain saw. He shows me where the flat boards are glued together into the general shape and size of Boniface, how he carved the body with the whining chain-saw blade.

Now he's going over every bit of it with a chisel. He will find the skin, the muscles, the expressions on his face. He will find the folds of fabric on his cloak, the strands of hair, the fingernails, the lashes of St. Boniface's eyes.

How were you trained for this? I ask him. I'm thinking of course of art schools, of sculpting classes in some city. I'm thinking of job searches and résumés and slides of his work. I'm thinking of how lucky he is to spend his days like this.

He's surprised by my question. No training, he says. His father did this, and his grandfather. He's been working with wood since he was seven. This is a discipline, a craft, his life.

His brother stands over by the window. He's working on a crucified Christ the size of a six-year-old. Again, the concentration and the chisel. He smooths the arms, the scalloped muscles in the thighs.

Behind the carver, there's a wooden Christ they've been using as a model for decades. You make him like this, like this. You turn him over, look at him from every angle to get the new one right. Does he ever work from living models? He says no, he doesn't. Does he think about what he's doing here? And he says he does, that there are days he thinks a lot about it. Though he does other things—cabinetry, wood patterns for the plastics industry, signs for chain stores, camcorder cases, television cabinets. Almost anything that's plastic was originally made in wood and then reversed and then reversed again.

What does he think on the days the carving suddenly seems eerie? He thinks that this is different. It's like a meditation. Some days it feels like nothing, some days like something spooky, some days like prayer. It's a privilege. It's a vocation. Some days he doesn't get it right, some days he does. All around him, there are Christs reclining on tables. They're all reclining, in some stage of abandon. When they're upright, some will be crucified Christs and some will be risen, depending on the church's focus—on the suffering in the second act or the joy in the third. Right now the risen are more popular, he says. It comes and goes.

He chisels the not-Christ from the surface of the wood, and it falls to the floor in curled white shavings. My days, my wasted days, what are they for. The carver smooths the wood. It's time to go, I say, I'm late. I'm drowning here. And they're waiting for me over at the factory.

Everything is hushed on the loading dock, and muffled in plastic. Not much to see.

My guide is at times Virgil, at times Charon, but he goes by the name Malik. He shows me to a white tram and ushers me into the passenger seat. Is it necessary? I ask. Please, I'd like to walk. Of course, he says, and he points the way, across an expanse of concrete, the open feel of a warehouse. How hard could it be to walk on your own power through a casket factory.

Malik is a sales rep, just out of college. I like him enormously. He'll do well, I think, and then he'll move into administration. Sales is no country for old men.

Through here, he says and motions to some stairs. I brace myself, put on protective plastic glasses, and walk through a metal door.

First there's the brilliant light, and then you hear the noise, the sound of falling scrap metal and the ka-thunk of die cast. Then the smell, like model airplane glue. This is the way you imagine a factory, all the complicated equipment and men with torches working with hot metal. They make the casket hardware out of alloys of zinc and aluminum. Scrap metal falls to the floor and disappears to reappear as something else. Nothing in a factory is wasted. All around there are stacks of bricks of silver-colored alloys like precious metals and bins of hardware waiting to be smoothed by man-made rocks.

Casket hardware has to look eternal. It has to be carefully made and carefully inspected. It has to be smooth to the touch. A good casket has to have hinges that won't allow the handles to rattle when the casket's being carried in a church. It has to have handles that pull up with a solid thud-like sound, like the sound built into the slamming of a car door, to signal the pallbearers that it's time to come forward. Good hardware has to not catch and unravel the clothes of the living.

Malik hands me hinges from a bin of hinges, handles from a bin of handles. This is good hardware, silver and shining.

Later on, some of the hardware will get a negative charge and in an instantaneous process will be coated with positively charged copper, like something from a science fiction movie, like some miracle. There's a flash in the air and all the silver metal in the glassed-in room turns gold. Alchemy. Resurrection.

Across from this room there's another windowed room where laborers take their breaks and smoke, the smoke like breath against the window, the spirit leaving the body in a puff. You would think that working all day on caskets would make you think, but most of the time it doesn't seem to.

There are times when the thought of death makes me physically shudder. It will come over me at the oddest times and for no real reason. The first time it did, I couldn't understand why people didn't talk about it constantly, why my friends didn't wake up each morning and call one another on the phone to remind ourselves we're going to die. There are days you can talk about death and it's like talking about salt or paper napkins. It's nothing. And other days when it seems so real that you can barely breathe. My friends who write seem to have those days more often. It's like the dark side of a mystical experience. It's like that negative charge in the copper-coating room. It's a physical start. It's unwilled, and it's painful. Who would ask for it? But it draws images to itself. Celine said that art is impossible without a dance with death.

So why am I here? I don't feel the shudder as much on this tour as I did earlier in the car or in the woodshop. I have a companion here, someone to talk to. Or perhaps it's just too much to think about. Perhaps it has to take you by surprise, like the grief you feel a month or year or several years or even decades after a loved one dies, more terrifying and real than anything you felt at the funeral. At any rate, caskets begin to seem so commonplace and strangely beautiful here—like finely crafted furniture or expensive cars—that occasionally I have to remind myself that what I'm looking at is mass-production housing for the dead.

Even 2,880 of them stacked in rows and filling an entire darkened room doesn't bring it home. Close to three thousand caskets, all resting on shelves stretching clear to the ceiling, waiting to be shipped, then chosen. This is the Triax area, the second largest Triax in the world, which means that in the center there's a giant robot that moves forward and backward, in and out, weaving among the caskets and lifting them from the shelves and bringing them over to where we're standing. No human beings touch them here. The more hands that have touched any product, the more opportunities for damage. Like love. Triax means the product is handled many times, but not by hand.

The goal is to ship a damage-free casket, a perfect casket. They test them in environmental chambers, they coat them with cathodic coating, they check each casket twice for a perfect seal. Each casket has to hold a vacuum for thirty seconds two different times before it leaves the factory. If it doesn't pass the test, it goes to a black light area where a man checks for microscopic holes.

There's a shaker that tests the casket with three hundred pounds of weight. They check the bottom well. The worst thing that can happen is a body falling out at a funeral. The bottom of the casket contains a bedspring and beneath that a liner. The bedspring holds the body even if the bottom were to fall, which it won't, but it also makes a place for corrosive fluids to drip from the body to the casket floor.

The caskets have warranties. Do people dig them up and check them? I ask and Malik says no, but there are times that the earth coughs them up—floods, in particular, and earthquakes—and there they are again. You want the caskets to remain intact. You want them to look nice. Like always wearing your good underwear in case you're in an accident.

The living don't want bodies floating up at them. The caskets have sealing mechanisms in the foot; when you die, you're vacuum packed. The sealing keeps out water and dirt and any other outside elements of the earth. This is the phrase you use in this business—not worms, not insects. Outside elements of the earth. A top-of-the-line casket will remain intact for seventy-five years. I thought they'd last forever. No, nothing does when it's buried, Malik explains, but the sealed metal casket comes close. It was introduced by this company in the 1940s, right before the war. Wooden caskets grew in popularity again in the 1960s, but even those, when they rot, become their metal liner. The skeleton of a wooden casket is a metal one.

But again, I'm talking about decay and fluid to make it sink in that this is a casket factory. When in fact it doesn't feel any more like a place for death than a furniture or toy store, than a warm restaurant on a Friday night, than your living room. You don't think of it. It's a place for living. I talk to men and women on the assembly line who have worked here thirty years and they seem happy. They have plans for retirement and lake cottages and vacations. How strange life is.

The main part of the factory is much like an automobile assembly plant. Rails move the silver metal caskets through the factory, matching the tops and bottoms, holding them with a mechanism suspended from the ceiling much like a monorail, swooping them down at times so that the caskets move from floor to waist to eye level to up above your head. The caskets are shiny and somehow cheerful, very much at this point looking like unlabeled vegetable cans.

There are men and women who check and turn the caskets, who watch over the machines, who seal and weld and sand them. A man in yellow rainboots and sunglasses runs a seam sealer. There's water on the floor underneath his boots, and his movements are the movements of a seamstress. When a robot's arm reaches the corner of a casket, the man yanks it quickly to get the perfect corner. The robot seals, the man yanks. Three yanks for each casket, and then it moves on down the line and another one replaces it.

Some of the caskets are machine sanded and some are sanded by hand. One hundred man-hours of sanding on each brass Prometheum, $25,000 or so for the finished product. There's a craftsman whose entire job is to do this. One by one, they're sanded, lined, and crated in a wooden box.

I'm fascinated by the cobalt blue welding flames, the way they reflect on the inner silver of the casket liners. They're beautiful, like gemstones. Don't look, Malik says, as I stand there staring at them. The welders pull visors over their eyes when the torch is on. Like the sun, the blue will damage the retina. They're already damaged, I tell my guide. I'm an eclipse-starer. Telling me not to look at something is a guarantee that my misbehaving eyes will be drawn to it.

All of the welders this day are men, but when you get into the paint and custom areas, there are more women. There's a woman who turns each casket on a swivel, checking the paint color after it's been through the paint room. Twenty-four different lead-free colors, but you can have a color custom-mixed and it will be shipped out in time for the funeral, usually in twenty-four hours. Last week, Malik says, someone sent in an IU red cap and had a casket tinted to match it. For some reason, that breaks my heart.

It had to be a man, I say, and he said yes that people do in fact choose caskets according to gender. Blues for men, white with brushed gold for a woman. The mauves and lavenders are good colors for women, Malik says, and the green can go either way. The polished stainless steel is beautiful and nongendered but definitely classed. They're expensive and they look that way, like a stainless steel Delorean. You can choose the interior, like an automobile ordered from the factory, and the interior colors look either masculine or feminine. Though I wonder what lasts of gender after the earth does its work. Perhaps a widening or narrowing of the pelvic cage, a bit of chromosome.

The interior is what you would see, if you could see, when the lid is shut, and it obviously won't matter. But funerals are for the living.

Oh, the custom interiors of a casket. Rows of women working on sewing machines. They work hard, and they chat and smile. Sister Carrie could have worked here, though these women are paid more and seem much happier. There are bolts of fabric hanging on racks, sitting on shelves. Any color you can imagine.

A popular custom interior for women is the wedding ring quilt. The quilts are hand-stitched by women in China. The quilts come packaged in plastic, and they're cut in strips by the casket factory workers and then re-sewn into liners, which, when they're placed in the caps that go into the lid, seem very much like an infant's bassinette.

The noncustom interiors are usually made of velvet and shirred on a machine or tailored.

You can have anything embroidered on a head dish. *Mother* is popular of course, and *grandmother,* but also birds and seals and flowers. The embroidery machine does five or six embroideries at once, from a pattern.

Malik shows me a pattern with three roses. There's a story behind this one, he says. After Rose Kennedy died, when the Kennedys went to the funeral home, they looked at a Batesville casket and also a competitor's. The funeral director called and said, you know, I think your casket's better, and if you could take that embroidered insert you have, the one with two roses, and somehow find a way to make a cap with three—one for each deceased son—I think they'll choose this one.

Overnight, they designed a dish with a third rose, and they sent it out. Rose Kennedy was buried in a

Batesville casket, and Bing Crosby and Sonny Bono and Frank Sinatra. Bill Clinton's mother and Hillary's father. Florence Griffith-Joyner is buried in a Batesville Persian Bronze. Phil Hartman's wife's cremains are buried in one of Batesville's urns. All these famous people, all these singular tragedies. None of this will appear in their advertising. They only mentioned this because I asked. Everything about the funeral industry is dignified and private.

And evolving. Malik shows me a small museum, a series of connected rooms that demonstrate the way caskets have been exhibited to the consumer. This is a re-production of the room the funeral director takes you to, apologetically, in the basement of the funeral home. The one where you make your selections, where you do your final shopping for your loved one. Would he like this stainless steel or this oak, this blue or green casket lining? If you haven't brought a sack of clothes, or if nothing in the wardrobe is suitable, or if there's been a long hospital stay and a change in size, you can buy clothing. Matronly looking mother-of-the-bride dresses for women, dark suits for men, all tying in the back like hospital gowns. You don't need to purchase shoes.

These rooms demonstrate to funeral directors how the consumer feels. Here in this mid-century post–world war room the panel and the carpeting are dark, stereotypically funereal, the kind of tone that translates into horror films. The caskets are arranged against the wall in such a way that you're afraid you'll fall into one, that one will topple down on top of you. In either case, it's frightening. It's sombre and as gray and orange as purgatory, the Hellenic hell. You don't want to linger here. You want to make your selection and move on up into the daylight.

Another decade and the lighting in the next model room is fluorescent, the walls are painted, the carpet still dark, but it's getting better. You feel that you're surfacing from something. You can see the skin of water up above you, you hope for air and light and then you break through, choking, and you're—in the 1990s room. There are halogen lights that give the room the warm blush of the living, and the colors are lighter, and the caskets are arranged somehow like bunk beds in a dormitory. And there's soft jazz playing somewhere, and the caskets are so plush and lovely that you wouldn't mind crawling inside of one for a temporary and communal restful sleep.

On the one hand, you feel as though this contemporary room will always and forever remind you more of living than of death, that there is something inherently peaceful in the colors and the music and the mood of the furnishings. On the other hand, you realize as you hear the salesman talk that you've been walking through what's nothing more than three decades' worth of changing taste, that the dark paneling and orange shag of the 1970s room was the dark paneling and shag of a 1970s living room. Which means that this particularly fashionable lighting and these particularly fashionable 1990s colors only give the illusion of the eternal, and they will seem as deathlike as ornate Victorian furniture a few short years into the twenty-first century. Fashion and style are always about keeping one step ahead of dying generations, the tasteless cars and floor-coverings of your parents, those reminders of your own mortality.

Outside the demonstration area there's a lobby filled with sculptures. I assume it's like sorbet between courses, like coffee beans in a fragrance shop, like saltine crackers during a test, that it's a place to rest. There are gorgeous mountains and deer scenes. Pine forests. Three aqua dolphins on a sculpted ocean. Extraordinary angels in clear acrylic, not looking trapped like insects look in amber but more like something taking form in smoke or fog or a beam of light or the colors that appear in polished diamonds.

Of course they're urns.

By the year 2010, I'm told, 50 percent of Americans will be cremated rather than buried. We want urns that look like pieces of fine art. We want our children to display them, and our grandchildren, and we don't want them to be ashamed. We don't want them to accidentally give these urns away or to hide them in a closet behind last winter's coat. There are places in the bottom of the urn where you seal all or a portion of the ashes.

They've done consumer studies, and this is what we want from death at this particular moment in Western history. We want trees planted in memory gardens. We want drawers so we can store memorabilia in the foot of our caskets. We want monograms. We want videochips in our headstones. When exercise and plastic surgery fail us, we want fire and ash, all clean and instantaneous but personal, all individual because the individual matters, after all, doesn't it? Don't we? Don't I? Me. I. We want the illusion of one individual casket or urn handcrafted by someone who loved me and will miss me desperately and eternally when I'm gone. One work of mass-produced art.

In the late Victorian era, when death was somehow still pre-industrial, photographers took final pictures of the dead sitting up in chairs and staring: like dolls, like wooden saints, they had painted-on eyes. There were advertisements for embalming fluid. Like this: Dr. Darr sits up in a chair, surrounded by his family. The caption reads: *Dr. Darr uses Frigidine Disinfectant Formaldehyde Compound. We will ship you a case of 6 gallons and if you're not satisfied after using 2 gallons, the balance can be returned. Like money in the bank! The persons viewing this picture and not knowing the circumstances would not be able to tell that Dr. Darr is deceased.*

The nineteenth century was also the beginning of cemeteries as gardens, the time of hair wreaths, the beginning of assembly-line caskets, which has its late twentieth-century flower in this factory here, in the town of B in Indiana. Death has always been both singular and universal, both the lingering death of your grandmother and the quick sharp death of the accident victim and the mass graves for the plague victims and the soldier. So many marked and unmarked graves, the few living at any time, the uncountable, anonymous, dead.

And so I've sailed the seas and come to this:

I get back in my car and leave the coffin factory. I think about the living people working there. I think about their pots and pans and their curtains and upholstered furniture and about the fireplaces waiting for them when they get off work, and about their food and books and music and about their churches and about their children. I think about the people I love so desperately. I think about their living eyes. Like kindling. Bless the life inside of them. Like kindling. Each holy minute, each blazing temporary minute. I'm sailing away now from Byzantium to take my place among the dying generations.

OPALESCENCE

The walls of the factory are century-old brick, rust-colored; the floors are uneven, the lighting dim. Outside, the sky is almost shockingly blue, and you can see a moon-shaped opalescent sliver of it through brown chinks in the ceiling or the occasional open door. Inside, it's as though you're walking through a dark, sepia-toned daguerrotype, all reddish-brown or black. When your eyes adjust to the dim, please look around.

First you see what looks like an abandoned room, someone's attic, filled with ancient rusted barrels and a table where the vice president of the company mixes recipes. The colors are written in italics in a leather book, some of them collaborations between the mixers' great-grandfather and Tiffany, the patron saint of colored glass: a rich cranberry, a cobalt blue, a green the mossy color of nineteenth-century satin dresses, a green that's almost black. Outside the recipe room there are more barrels filled with chunks of cullet glass, cast-offs, broken pieces you mix with other broken pieces to get new colors made here inside the chipped brick walls and high black ceilings, under the dimmest lights. The most beautiful opalescent iridescent colors from barrels of glass chunks, word clots, river stones, whatever you imagine.

Don't go inside that door without a mask.

Yes, that one with the board across the top, the one you have to duck through. Just bend down and peer. It's where ingredients are mixed, where the forklifts cross back and forth and the bass on the booming radio is turned up and the air is filled with white dust and the men wear masks across their faces and there are boxes and wagons filled with swirling silica sand and feldspar, soda ash, and lime. Everything is covered with the stuff like snow or broken sacks of flour—the windows, the floor and walls, the men's hair and arms—the dry particulate matter that in this form dulls and obscures but that will, shortly, be melted into something you can see through.

And be careful where you walk. Cold glass will cut. Hot glass will burn.

Instead, follow me through here, inside this room. It's extraordinarily hot, and it's as dark as a basement except there, across the room, where there are two white furnaces shaped like igloos.

In each furnace there are twelve portals less than a foot across and each one of the holes is glowing absolutely as bright and orange as the sun—every bit as bright.

It's like someone has built a white hut and filled it with some kind of hot soup directly from the sun, a big flaming kettle of sun, a large pot of molten lava. The sun is here, in the middle of a tiny factory in Kokomo, Indiana; they've found some way to mine it, some mystic pipeline, right across the street from Delphi. And if you wear glasses for safety, they'll let you look straight into it. The sun.

There's a man with a long ladle, like a soupspoon, and he sticks the ladle into the kettle of the sun and brings out a great glowing orange-neon globe of it, a new sun, a new star. And he runs with it, from the kettle to a metal table; about twenty feet he runs carrying this ladle of melted glass that weighs close to a hundred pounds. And as he runs, he pops the glass to keep the cooling even, pitching it an inch or two above the ladle and catching it, a little like jai alai—maybe, the ball and the wicker cesta, only in this case the ball is pure orange plasma, and the cesta iron. And the arena is simply the dusky dim light of the factory, all black and rust, with this one amazing flaming ball popping its way across the night sky, a meteor.

He pours the star out onto the table where it oozes into a flat disk, like certain kinds of dough, and another man turns it with a spatula, and if this batch of glass is going to be multicolored another man brings an identical-looking molten mass from the kettle and adds it, and then another, and the mixer stirs and pushes it toward a roller like one of those taffy machine rollers you watch through a window in some tourist beach town. At this stage, and when it dries, the process seems much in fact like candy-making. You want to touch it, but it's been melted in a 2,500-degree oven.

And the unreal stuff—this melted silica and feldspar and soda ash and lime, this proof that matter can be transformed, that bodies can be resurrected, that the great joy of the universe is in this constant changing—comes out flat on the other side of the roller and moves into another room where, in the melting, the miracle happens. The teal appears. The reds and yellows and blues and greens and indigos and violets. It's as flat and transparent and as smooth and lovely as hard candy, and it will cut your fingers if you touch its edges.

There are four men who pop the glass. They take turns running with the ladles. They run four, then take a break. It's a relay, and they work eight-hour shifts, six days a week. They place the ladles in the kettle, they run, they dump the doughy molten glass, they sit back on a bench that looks like the time-out box that hockey players sit in.

Every minute and a half the bell rings; it's someone's time to run. This is no job for old men. You run with the hot ladles, and you hope you don't fall and that you're not too slow and that your arms will hold. Some of the lava drips along the floor as you run and hardens on contact. So you walk back to your seat on strings and fragile threads of green and yellow glass, like threads of sugar. That's when you know what color you've been carrying.

There are twelve ceramic pots inside the furnace, each filled with a different colored batch. The pots are made in brick kilns along another wall. Each time they change colors, they clean the pots. The clay pots, like large flowerpots without holes, last for fifteen to twenty weeks and then need to be replaced. They only make black glass when it's time to change the pots because the color is so dense that it's impossible to clean. Between every other color, they scour the pots with melted glass. They use the yellow glowing stuff like sandpaper.

Only the strongest, most experienced men replace the pots. It's dangerous work.

The furnace can't be let to cool; it takes too long to get it up to speed. So the men put on three or four sweatshirts and a mask and gloves, and they tear the brick front from the furnace with pikes and the gas flames shoot out at them and a fireproof curtain lowers from the ceiling and they drive a fresh hot cherry pot from the kiln over on a fork lift and they get as close as they can to the fire and ease the pot inside. If they're too close to the fire for more than fifteen seconds, their skin will burn.

They rebuild the furnace with long pikes, all the masonry work done quickly; again, the timing has to be perfect, and everyone's yelling at everyone because it's so dangerous and fast and at the end they hurl wet clay at the chinks like grenades. They can see the awe in people's faces when they tour the factory. They know that this place that makes the colors for cathedral windows is in itself a kind of cathedral, that a painting of them, if done right, would have a kind of mystery and terrifying power. But they envy the men who work in the warehouse—it's an easier life boxing up the colored glass in crates filled with wood shavings.

The two men on the other side of the roller, the ones who welcome the sheets of glass into the world, are part of the same relay as the men who pop the glass. Now and then one runs toward the Coke machine. The universe is timed exactly. Everything has meaning. He's got one and a half minutes to get a soft drink and get back to his place at the end of the table. One second late and the entire sheet of glass shatters on the floor.

They wear odd polymer canvas sleeves, covered with stainless steel buttons, that attach at the chest. They pull the glass toward them. They don't, by tradition, cover the belly. The arteries that can be cut are in the arms.

They cut the glass into perfect rectangles. They throw the excess glass into the hog. The tour guide can't talk above the sound of breaking glass. All around you, for the rest of the tour, there will be sheets of glass taller than you are. You have to be careful where you walk. The edges are sharp. As much as you'd love to touch the colors, you can't, though the tour guide will bring a small bit of it to you so you can feel the texture the glass picked up from the flattening stone in the annealing process, so you can look through the watery translucent parchment. The waves and marks are called tablemarks. They make each plate different, like handmade paper. The artist who forms the glass, later, will work with the marks, the grooves. Often, they'll inspire him or her. Twentieth-century Kokomo glass transluces exactly like nineteenth-century glass. Because of the size of the business, because of the twelve-pot furnace, because they do things the same way they did one hundred years ago, they make more varieties of colors—18,000 combinations of color, density, texture, with 288 core colors, and they can mix others by hand.

You've walked through the heat and fire and furnace, the darkness and the place your sins are turned to steam, to glass—first darkly, that obscuring dust, that heat that burns, that gorgeous suffering, then later, face to face. Before you leave, stand here and walk down this hallway, this glimpse of paradise. Sheets of extraordinary color are filed against the wall. The glass sheets are arranged by number, by color, and by texture. The glass glows, truly, like a box full of jewels in the sunlight from the clear glass window, like melted crayons between waxed paper. But not quite that. You can only gesture toward what you sense here, not get it quite.

Here you can walk into and through the light from a cathedral window: into cobalt, into rose, into lavender and creamy yellow, into rhododendron and forsythia, into ocean, into mountain stream, into forest, into glacial ice, into the stars, the moon, into opals and garnets, into emeralds and sapphires, into diamonds, into the light and color from everything translucent and shining. You can walk between the rows of glass like you walked into your wedding picture.

But it's not time for you yet. Stay right there in the middle. Don't get too close. It's fragile and delicate and now and then a sheet of glass will shatter unexpectedly, just fall to the floor from the weight of perfection balanced against this gravity. Angel wings, the iridescent wings of dragonflies. It used to be that iridescence was created by spraying the cooling glass with fly insecticide. Now they spray it with some secret something that's far less dangerous.

This is a family, closed-stock business, the largest manufacturer of art glass in the world. Its history resides in one italics-filled book. It's surrounded by enormous divisions of Chrysler-Daimler and Delphi Electronics. The Chrysler employees received huge bonuses last week and are spending them, according to the newspaper, on motorcycles. Which they'll use to fly through this place in search of something that's someplace else.

Meanwhile, at the glass company in the corporations' shadows, they know that whatever they use to make the iridescence was invented three Bill Wrights ago. There has been a Bill Wright making cathedral and opalescent glass right in this spot for over one hundred years. How could this be? How could it not be? What keeps him in this place in these different bodies? What does Bill Wright see through these jewel-like windows? Day after day, year after year. The sun rises. The sun sets. One translucent body formed from light. The breakage. The molten sun. The new sun forming. And on and on. This path to eternity: this fabrication of strange beauty. It's there around you always if you look for it. Opalescence. This standing forever in one place.

AND SO I HASTEN TO
TAKE THIS OPPORTUNITY

My dearest:

Since I am rapidly growing older every day I live, I hasten to take this opportunity to ask you to be mine.

I assure you that I can make bread and fry potatoes.

I will refrain from performing on the piano.

I believe I have every qualification for a good wife.

—Wisconsin woman, 1899

I'm trying not to eavesdrop, I swear, but their conversation is louder than they think it is. They're in their own world and quite unaware of anything outside of it. And they're talking about sex.

You feel it drawing their attention, no matter what else they try to talk about. It's magnetic. It's a loom that draws everything else into it. It creates meaning, like any obsession. You hate to let it go.

Of course it's hard to see around desire. It will never end, you hope, not once, not ever. Heads will always turn when you walk into a room.

Everywhere they go, it seems, or so they say, someone is hitting on them.

Hitting on them. It sounds like hail.

As far as I can tell, the women are old college friends. At least one of them went to medical school and one of them is married, with a child, working as a postdoc in something. The third one seems to be a businesswoman. The child is sitting at the table. I can't be more exact than that because I really don't know them. They're eating Indian food. I'm eating Thai. The man at the table next to mine is eating pizza and a bowl of soup.

We're all listening to the women as they talk around the child.

All three women are, as one of them comments, *hotter* than any of the men they know. They're wearing tight black pants, they have gorgeous hair, they're all around twenty-six or seven, and they're surrounded by shopping bags. They run miles every day, I hear them talking about it, and they're very conscious of what they eat. No red meat, ever, and very little sugar.

They're more beautiful than they were in college. They're more beautiful than they have ever been. They radiate self-conscious energy and power. It feels limitless to them.

The mall we're sitting in is filled with Prada bags and plastic fish, with everything we need or ever will; objects—even cabinet pulls—fetishized with futuristic green glass lights, fake rocks, and shining oak so you want them. Each object has a setting, seems to point toward some utopian fabricated life. At one entrance there's a four-foot high sculpture made of chocolate.

This mall is so huge there's a disembodied voice that tells you, when you enter, that it's door eighteen you've entered, over and over you're entering door eighteen. The voice is that Disney voice.

Indian food, Chinese food, American, Thai, Italian, pretzels dusted with cinnamon and sugar, crushed ice mixed with kiwi from New Zealand. My mother made a daily cake or pie from scratch, without a mix; my own daughter has hardly ever seen me in the kitchen. My grandmother made dresses with her own patterns; my mother used tissue paper patterns; I can barely sew a button on. My daughter wants to buy a new shirt when the button's missing and throw the old one out.

Move fast. My kids sit at the computer carrying on fifty conversations at once. AOL Instant Messages blossom on the monitor like the grand finale of the century's biggest fireworks show, complete with lights and sound, new language hardwired into their brains, who has time for capitals or punctuation. n-e-way. This is the place where life feels possible. This is the place where you feel your spirit lift. This is the place that feels like church should feel but doesn't.

Wisconsin, 1999. A mall in the middle of pine trees and dairy country, the whole thing geared now for tourists.

The married one just got invisible braces on her teeth. One of the single women had them years ago. They were just like yours, she says; my braces were behind the teeth, inside the mouth.

She explained how, when you had oral sex, it could be very painful for the guy.

I was thinking that, the married woman said. Even in my situation.

The guy at the table next to mine chokes on his pizza but recovers. His soup is steaming. Honestly.

The black-haired woman seems to be from out of town. She's staying with her married friend.

Last night the married woman watched out the window as her friend came in late, driven by a male colleague, and sat out in the driveway, making out. It was just recreational, she said, something fun. She had no feelings for the guy beyond friendship.

You learn how to do it with the braces, she says. You have to suck it back into your throat without touching your palate, and you use your lips.

She's the one I think is a physician. There are other clues besides this one, which is, I admit, not much of a clue. It has to do with words: fellow, med center, and with the way she carries herself, and the fact that she knows the generic name for Sudafed, which is, she explained to her friends, a diet pill. It dries you out, she says, and makes you thirsty. You drink a lot and don't want to eat.

I'm full, the married woman says, somehow in response. Her plate is filled with creamed spinach and curried cauliflower. Her daughter is eating white rice and a pack of refined white sugar. I'll let her have just one, the mother says, referring to the packet.

You know, the businesswoman says, looking at the child, I read in yesterday's *New York Times* that the uterus muscle turns white when it expels the fetus. Is this true? So many women used to die that some famous somebody said he'd toyed with the idea that female mammals were meant to have one child and then expire, like insects.

That's not probable, the mother said; it would be some kind of evolutionary suicide. Who would take care of the children?

The second wife, the physician said. Or the third or fourth or fifth one. You've seen those nineteenth-century cemeteries. Women were constantly replaced. You wonder why those women got married at all. It had to feel like some sort of virgin sacrifice.

Thank God it's 1999, one says. This becomes a refrain, as in Thank God it's 1999, or After all, it's 1999 or Come *on,* it's 1999.

It's a Saturday, you're shopping with your friends and all this glittery merchandise is calling you. Where could life be better?

Though there's now and then a vague feeling of unease. We all feel it. You know that anything you buy is old before you get it home. Maybe the lighting's wrong. You head back out for more. But no. *Outdated.* The new furniture in your home is nostalgic for some mid-twentieth-century forward-looking Jetsons modernism. You paid an arm and a leg for it. You want it to look young at least for a year or two into the coming millennium. Please dear God. One second to breathe.

You don't know where all the stuff that fills this mall is coming from. You don't know what sustains it, or why you deserve it, if you do.

Now and then you have looming nightmares of the nighttime skies filled with silent, fascist metal birds. The hulls are as long as football fields, two stories high. They're stuffed with things, and the air is solid with them, the surreal version of passenger pigeons. They fly around the skies all night delivering things to you, and not just shoes but food. You don't know why that nightmare vision terrifies you. Maybe it's the fact that it's anonymous and large and whatever supports it is invisible and out of your control.

You actually know someone who's been to the world economic conference in Switzerland. He was there by invitation. It was, he said, the creepiest thing he's ever seen. It made him want to hide inside his home.

Everyone is there, he says, all the leaders, and it's all surreal. Gates and Bill and Hillary. The United Nations is for tourists, he says, but no leader misses the economic conference. Tiny third world countries. Everyone is there. Limousines, giant dishes filled with iced shrimp, the finest wines. Who wouldn't want to be a part of it, finally? It's such a feast. The leaders who are old school get bombed for a while for what is ostensibly the holiest of reasons. The next year they're brought into the fold.

It's like an academic conference, your friend says, but the men go to panel discussions about how to rule the world. Their wives listen to gurus talk about new age spirituality. They know just how many artists a community needs, how much this and how much that.

It's easy to rule the world, your friend says. And fun. It's not much different from making a simulated computer city. Put in this mall, this road, this balloon stand, get it absolutely right, and suddenly the screen will be filled with little Sims, walking, all of them the same.

Do they ever ask where this apple came from? This rice? This bowl of soup? Perhaps. You don't own a seed, a sprig of grass, you couldn't make anything if your life depended on it, you live ten stories high in an apartment in Chicago. Everything you need you have to buy, and the thing you buy it with is more and more surreal.

There's a holographic bird on the corner of your credit card. In the right light, it hovers an inch or two above the plastic. You've somehow tied your fate to it.

This morning an iron you bought two weeks ago broke while you were using it. The commercials aimed at children, your friend says, are starting to make him sick.

Don't think about it.

I do some quick and painful math. The anonymous Wisconsin woman was born three generations before me. I could have been her great-granddaughter. The three women at the table were born at least twenty years after me. They could be my daughters. But in some ways I'm close to equidistant between the two. It's an oddly distant place to hover. Everyone seems sweetly deluded, everything a crumbling, fragile fabrication, the way every age seems from the one you're standing in. *Let the old dead make way for the young dead.* So this is the new world. Let the old one go.

Now and then the little girl becomes the focus of everyone's attention. One gets her a napkin, another gets her bread. I like that they do this. They love the little girl, though the single women's response to the girl's mother is subtly condescending. As though she's missing out on some great adventure, has made some extraordinarily foolish choice, like using heroin or having unprotected sex. The mother, I know, is wondering this same thing. As though she cut the whole thing off too soon, as though she'd signed up for some voluntary servitude. Though she wouldn't trade her little girl for anything. It's only her friends who make her feel this way. Maybe she won't be with the girl's father long. Though it's so expensive, duplicating everything for the child. She'll need a different job. Two bedrooms, two televisions, two phone lines, two beds and dressers, two sets of clothes.

Try this, the physician says to the girl, or this. All children like lentils.

The little girl doesn't like lentils. She hates them. She puts her head down on her plate and quietly refuses them.

Just eat one bite of something good for you, her mother whispers, and you can have one of these. She takes a plastic bag from her purse. She takes it from her purse with shame and furtiveness. The bag is filled with processed, round, stamped cookies. The girl takes the cookies from the bag and begins eating them. Two at a time, her hands are soon covered with gummed-up cookie mess, crumbs, and saliva. The cookies may as well be made by elves in hollow trees, they appear that magically. I've given so many of them to my own children. What have I taught them that's of any worth?

Like you'd follow a river, I follow that cookie to its source.

Such a strange juxtaposition, these tiny cookies and this machinery, these enormous coffinlike bins of dough, the women with the little girl sitting at the mall eating these cookies from a Ziploc see-through bag.

The machine that makes these cookies is so large the ingredients are weighed. No cups, no spoons marked with a T or t. There are thick pipes on the ceiling that read Sugar, Shortening, Flour, and Fine Oat Crush. The recipe may change as the characteristics of one year's wheat harvest changes. But Larry, the man who controls the pipes, never tastes the dough; not like a cook, he's more like a mechanic. He adds more sugar not because of how the dough tastes but because of how it looks and mixes.

It doesn't seem to matter really how the cookies taste. You pay premium prices for the illusion of home-baked cookies. These are the cookies children take in lunches; they taste like sugary cardboard, truly.

It only matters how the cookies look and how they're packaged and how they're marketed and that they don't break. Cookies are made and packaged in one factory for many different brands and then they're shipped around the world to supermarkets. Same cookies, different boxes. Your local brand was not made locally. There are no elves.

But there are troughs of chocolate-colored stuff—troughs and troughs of it—and barrels of jelly and sugar.

Women work the lines. They pack the cookies in boxes and bags. They watch the peanut butter fall between two wafers. The wafers run in a line that splits in two and rotates. Two thousand sandwiches per minute, sixteen per row. All day long, tiny butter cookies and wafers. The women stand and watch them being made. There's no flour on their clothing, no children at their feet. They check the color of the cookies against a color chart. They lift out broken ones. They pat the plastic sacks to make sure they're filled with air as well as cookies, and they check the nozzles. They pack the boxes into bigger boxes. You picture those scenes of women on the lines during the world wars, making bullet shells.

The butter cookies are shaped like a child's drawing of a flower, and a stream of them falls into barrels before they're packed in sacks with pictures of the mascots of whatever company the cookies are being sent to.

The cookies are almost impossible to break. They fall several feet into the barrels, the sacks of them will make cross-country trips on trucks, they'll fall off grocery store shelves and ride in the bottom of trunks of cars, they'll end up in plastic bags at the bottom of children's backpacks, some other child will sit on them on the school bus, and still they won't break.

The cookies never just sit in a warm oven and rise toward heaven. They're baked in batches of 1,800 and 2,000 pounds, and they're constantly in motion. The ovens are two hundred feet long, and the cookies will bake in five to seven minutes.

Five to seven minutes. There's a difference in the leavening systems you use to make a cookie in a factory and there's a difference in the molecular structure of the cookie itself; they're more acidic, which helps with the shelf life. They won't mold or get stale. They're eternal cookies.

Rolls of cookie dough are cut with a disk, a wire, or a guillotine, depending on the cookie.

Fruit bars are extruded, they ooze out of tubes, the jams and the jackets.

I've worked here twenty years, one man says. He wears khaki pants and a blue shirt. There are men and women wearing dark expensive suits. The ones in suits are self-important. They live in cities.

Those guys, he says, pointing to the ones in suits, don't know a damn thing about cookies. What they know is something else.

These women, he says, pointing to the women on the line, they know the cookies. Something goes wrong with these machines, they fix them. They make sure we weigh each box to check for accidental error, we scan them with electric eyes, we're careful and safe and efficient. They know when the color's wrong, the way the cookies are supposed to taste by how they look. They eat these cookies all day long. I wish they tasted better.

The women in this morning's shift, I notice, are mostly older. They're the ones who have seniority. In the evening shift it's different, he says. The husbands are home to watch the kids, and the younger women come to work then. Sometimes these first shift women moonlight as babysitters for the second shift. The first-shift looks after the second one. They get along. On the weekends they watch their husbands sing karaoke at the Eagles Lodge. Sometimes they join in.

My guide was at the University of Wisconsin in the sixties. He was in the building that was blown up, then filled with tear gas. How were those days? I ask him. The most exciting of my life, he says, but we were all, every one of us, half crazy. I'm glad, he says, that it's all behind me.

Sometimes you live in this vivid sunlight, and then something violent happens, he says, and then you live in this haze, grateful for it. You tend to stay grateful for the haze. Younger people think you've sold out, he says. My kids do. When in fact you're just taking care of them, until they're through the craziness. And you're glad, yourself, to be out of it.

The factory light is fluorescent. There are no windows. He's inside all day long.

Do you eat the cookies yourself? I ask. Of course, he says, we eat them all the time. The sugar draws you in, it's an addiction. It blocks out every other taste. I supposed if the cookies tasted better, it would be much worse.

Do you ever bake? I ask him and he says no, none of us do. There's no reason to. You can take home boxes and sacks of cookies anytime you want to. At the end of the day, we've worked two shifts, we're too tired to bake, we don't even want to cook. You eat this much sugar and you seem to lose the taste for everything.

Halfway across the country there's a factory that makes communion wafers. It uses this same machinery. Vats of dough and an assembly line and a disk that stamps the dough into tiny bread-shaped wafers. No leavening, no sugar. They're shipped in anonymous boxes to church supply warehouses and then to trusting human tongues. The sugars in the mouth begin to break the wafer down. They have no intrinsic flavor. You wouldn't choose to eat one outside this context.

Will you help plant and harvest the wheat? Will you bake the bread or churn the butter? Could you do it if you needed to? Not I, not I, not I. I'm too damn busy.

Everyone's skin looks gray to me, I think, and pasty, though maybe it's the light. You can pick up a cookie from anywhere you look. This batch is enrobed with a deep brown drizzle. It's some waxy something that looks like chocolate and tastes like nothing. Whatever it is falls like rain onto the lines of wafers. Take this. Eat. This strange communion. No wonder desire seems less of a sacrament. Who's running this show? Is it good or evil or simply something else?

Whatever it is, it's happening quickly. It's all around you, and you can't quite see outside of it. The constant downpour of this fabricated something.

ARCADIA

On the first day of October, I set out in search of Arcadia and ended up, instead, in Hobbs. To get to Arcadia, you take the first right after Omega. The second right out of Omega leads to Delphi.

At the edge of Omega I saw a blue tractor and two white swine. I saw a pumpkin wind sock with a black bat. I saw the road to Delphi. I didn't see a sign for Arcadia and so I ended up, as I said before, in Hobbs.

I didn't mind. It was the first day of October. In October I don't regret things. It's the only month, in fact, that I don't regret not living by the ocean. There are days in October when it seems there's been some kind of strange inversion, that you're walking through an atmosphere of sun and yellow pollen and the sky is actually a great blue ocean up above your head and you can hear it roaring, and the sound seems to hold you inside something secure and good.

I had no compelling reason to go to Arcadia other than its name. It seemed like the right thing to be doing in October. And I'd left my desk and headed out into the country because it was the kind of beautiful day you should dedicate to whimsy. So I turned off the highway. In October you can look for Arcadia and find Hobbs and know that, in fact, you've found what you were looking for.

From the highway, the factory looked like a steaming boiler, a pressure cooker on an old wood-fired stove, a bit ramshackle, a bit down on its luck, beyond quaint. It was a small canning factory, a silver-gray, flat-roofed building with a propane tank toward the road and black pipes and tubes and steam.

I expected the canning process to go on inside the building. I expected the Tim-Burtonesque pounding dark of factories. I expected heat. I expected some terrifying and strange contrast between vegetable and machine. I expected some slaughterhouse for tomatoes, filled with knives and fire and oozing tomato flesh, some contrast to the cool air and the October light and the enormous sky. I expected an antidote to all the sunlight, a pleasant shiver. I expected the usual.

As I drove around the building, the first thing I saw was a row of open-bed trucks mounded with tomatoes. There were at least five large trucks, all of them brimming with rich red. It wasn't the greenish-pink ironic orange I expect from a truck of fresh-picked tomatoes. I know what to do with pinkish-orange. I don't even know now what to say when faced with this much ripeness. All the thoughts I might usually have don't even occur to me. You see? Arcadia. A place of innocence. Right there in Hobbs.

Next to the trucks there was a compound of small buildings, and on the front of one of them a sign: *Hobbs Cafeteria: Home Cooked Meals.* It was an excuse for me to stop the car, to just blend in to the place and not have to go up to the office, explain what I was doing there, what I was looking for, which was and is even now almost impossible.

The cafeteria was a long, rectangular room lined with windows, a room on one end of an old building that had at one time served some other purpose—canning, labeling. It was completely functional. No curtains, no pictures on the wall. There were about six picnic tables at one end, like a cafeteria in a small grade school where everyone plans on sitting together and then getting back to work.

I should have known that this wasn't a real cafeteria. There was no sign of a menu, nothing to indicate what there was to order, just a counter with an ancient, elaborately molded brass cash register and two black-haired women working around a stove. One of the women was opening jars and setting napkins in a holder, and the other was wrapping tortillas around meat sauce and placing them in a metal roasting pan.

I asked if they had sandwiches, and both women smiled at me. I took the smile as a no and asked what was on the menu. The women continued smiling. I smiled back. We all smiled until one of the women seemed to feel sorry for me and said, Enchiladas. I took this to mean that I was supposed to order enchiladas, and I asked how much. One dollar, she said, with rice and beans.

It wasn't until then that I realized this was not a restaurant people just come to from off the highway, that the factory was a self-contained economy and these enchiladas were to serve the workers. I tried to explain that I was sorry, that I hadn't understood. I tried to leave. But they piled a plate with hot food and I handed them a dollar and bought some sweet lemonade-laced tea for a quarter, and they smiled again and said in Spanish that they didn't speak English and I said in English that I didn't speak Spanish and we grinned until our faces hurt, all of us meaning well and saying *Enchiladas,* one of the only words, in addition to *tea* and *gracias* and *hello* and *how much* and *rice and beans* and *thank you,* that we were quite certain all of us understood.

I've lived in the industrial Midwest all of my life. I remember my great-grandmother speaking German, but she's been dead for forty years. That's the last time I remember hearing someone in Indiana who wasn't in a classroom, speaking a language that wasn't English in a practical "you're hungry and here's food" rather than a "what if you were in Spain and you were hungry and wanted food" way. I had driven from the mall-encrusted homogeneity of the city out into the country and what I thought I'd see was a kind of nineteenth-century Midwest peopled with characters out of James Whitcomb Riley. I didn't expect to drive thirty miles north of Indianapolis and end up in Mexico or Texas, but I have. It's October, and this world is changing. The tomatoes are ripe. I'd driven to Arcadia. But I didn't speak the language and the food was unfamiliar and somehow I didn't belong there.

There was no difference in the temperature between outside the cafeteria and in, absolutely none at all. There was a slight breeze and that extraordinary yellow sunlight and that blue sky and that brilliant red fruit. The thing about October light is that it makes things more vivid, absolutely themselves.

Attached to the left of the factory there was a metal roof covering a loud confluence of machines. The color of the tomatoes being dropped from a truck into a bin drew me over to them. I stood in the drive, about five feet away from the complicated web of machinery, watching the color red as it dropped from the truck to a mesh sorter and began to jump and roll down tubes and into tubs and up through other tubes, disappearing into the factory.

I tried to follow a single tomato to see how the process worked, though it was of course impossible and counterproductive finally. It caused me to *direct* my sight when what I wanted was to be directed by something.

What I wanted was to end up someplace I didn't expect to be when I started this.

And in fact I wasn't as interested in the process as in the color red and in the juice and in the sheer spectacle of tumbling tomatoes, more amazing in their way than anything I could travel great distances to see.

I couldn't imagine how you could ever be unhappy there. It felt like a place I'd been banished from for some now-forgotten crime. Perhaps something I didn't even stop to recognize had come too easily, without much sacrifice on my part and for some at too much cost.

Just as I was thinking this, a middle-aged man in a red hat walked over a metal scaffolding from one side of the tomato sorter to another. He had the lanky, gray-haired look of a farmer. I expected to see him here, but I was afraid he was going to be angry. I was afraid he would think I was a terrorist or an inspector looking for illegal migrant workers, or that I was a crazy person. I was afraid there wouldn't be a language we could speak to one another across whatever suspicious distances there can be between human beings.

But he walked over and stood beside me and commented on the weather. I pointed to the tumbling tomatoes and told him they were beautiful. I hoped his assumption about me would be that I was a simple, harmless crazy woman out for an autumn drive and that he would let me stay until I had seen all I'd come here to see, whatever that was.

The tomatoes disappeared into what looked like washtubs, and they appeared on a conveyor on the other side. They ran under a chartreuse light then, and a juice made of seeds and pale green and reddish-orange liquids fell onto the concrete floor. I assumed the liquid was a combination of overripe smashed tomatoes and some kind of soap and that the tubs in front of me were where the fruit was cleansed before canning, but I wasn't sure, so I asked him.

He took a step toward the machine, and I thought he was ignoring me because he had work to do, something important to inspect or adjust. Instead he put his hand under a waterfall of tomatoes and came back with one perfect oblong piece of red fruit.

He explained that the bins were a lye bath that took the skin off the tomatoes. It was lye and skin raining down on the concrete. The round meat of the tomato lay in his hand like a heart, like throbbing sunlight, and he slid it into my hand where it felt alive and warm and much heavier than I expected.

The chartreuse light sorted the ripe from the unripe, the quick from the dead.

And the canning goes on inside the building? I asked sweetly, indirectly, midwesternly.

And he said, Come inside and see.

He didn't ask my name, what I was doing there, why I cared. There was a sense in which, through language and culture, he already knew me.

Five miles away from Hobbs, right outside of Wind-fall, there was a tent show billed as a once-in-a-millennium event. I had gone there earlier in the morning. It was the Farm Progress Show, an annual trade show that moves among the "I" states, that part of the industrial United States that thinks of itself as agricultural. Dr. Jekyll and Mr. Hyde. This is what I am, and this is what I appear to be. The more I hide what I am, the more sentimental I become about the mask.

To get to the trade show, you drive on a road lined with row after row of labeled corn. A three-dimensional, living, breathing, billboard for seed. Dekalb. Pioneer. This corn was so close to the road and so dense, and the road so white and narrow and so empty, that for a moment or two, as I drove there, I felt claustrophobic, that overwhelming panic that pioneers described when they felt closed in by the tall grass of the prairies. I had a car phone, and I almost called home, the panic was that great. Talk me through this, please, some familiar reassuring voice reaching in here from outside of this, some distant point of orientation, not this terrifying quiet voice of God inside the coffin, be still and follow. No, don't take me, please. If I could only see above this, grab hold of something on the other side of this, I would feel safely rooted in this sweet October.

The tall-grass pioneers felt this panic as drowning, felt the movement of the wind on the bluestem as oceanic. But my panic felt more like an injection of ether or, rather, like helium in the blood or a strong wind, something that threatened to lift or fling me up into that beautifully opaque and airless sky.

On the four-lane superhighway where I usually travel, the stalks of corn are at a distance, behind a fence, alternating with red, unthreatening beans. I can usually see the horizon. For better or worse, that's the landscape I'm used to, and my whole coherent sense of both reality and identity are more closely tied to the familiarity of that landscape than I'd imagined.

As I got near the trade show, beyond the wall of showy corn, there was a leveled field of cut, white stubble, where I could feel the scattered particles of my self come back together into something I could recognize as me.

I've lived my entire life in a city or on roads between towns and cities. I very seldom fly, and I very seldom camp or walk through woods. This is a confession. A year ago I stayed for four days at a camp in southern Indiana, and I walked in uncut country for the first time since, I'm ashamed to admit, my childhood. Walking through the grass at the edge of the woods, I was struck by the uncertainty, the way that solid footing disappeared beneath layers of vegetation, the hidden mounds and rocks and roots and unexpected dips. I was struck by the amount of concentration it took to walk, by the heart-pounding and sudden scurrying-away of animals I couldn't see or even begin to name. I was struck by the heat and the moisture and the way I had trouble breathing in the thick pollen. I was struck by the shrill green incessant insects, the way hundreds of them were dislodged with every step: crickets and flies and, in the boggy places, the creepy silence of those bottle-blue-colored flying twigs, whatever they're called, and dragonflies, with their weblike decayed-leaf transparent wings. I was struck by how easy it was to lose my way, by how often I calculated the distance back and wondered how fast I could run from some human or nonhuman terror hiding behind the next oak tree.

When I drove back home to the city, I felt relief. I walked across a strip mall parking lot and didn't miss the crickets. I thanked God for asphalt and air-conditioning and clean, well-lighted restaurants. I thanked God for grocery stores and nursing homes and hidden slaughterhouses and cemeteries. I thanked God for the veneer, the human cradle, the safety, the familiar. The womb of culture.

From a half mile away, I could see the tents of the Farm Progress Show. It had been a dry summer. The footing where I parked my van was dried-out, dusty soil mixed with shiny purple tubes of fallen corn.

For the three days of this trade show, this temporary town is one of the largest, measured by either area or population, in the state of Indiana. It's a grid of tents and ephemeral streets that run from First to Tenth intersected by streets with unpoetic names: Central, Capital, and South. Block after block of seeds and machinery, amazing in their warlike scale, like tanks and planes—the way you have to climb up ladders to enter them, the blue bubble of glass over the cockpits, the language used to describe them: pressure flow, compensated hydraulics, clutch, and speed and power. Everywhere there were tasteful quiet experts and slogans: *Pioneer delivers genetics the way you want them.*

Ninety-nine percent of the faces were white faces floating under a sea of green caps. These were the grandchildren and great-grandchildren of an earlier migration—Scotch-Irish, German, British, French. Willa Cather pioneers. Children had the day off from the consolidated county schools, and they threw footballs at the FFA exhibit and talked to recruiters from Purdue, and their faces were the optimistic open faces of the fathers and mothers, but they were dressed like kids from any American city—sweaters from Gap and Abercrombie and Old Navy. And you somehow also knew, from their expressions, that they were the sons and daughters of successful businessmen. Their faces were like the faces of television-raised city children, mall children, the faces of consumers. And you knew that they would prefer the industrial repetition of a summer job at McDonald's—the uniforms, the grill, the shining chrome—to farmwork. You knew they expected something good from their lives, perhaps something not very difficult. You knew they wouldn't be staying here when they were through high school and that their sweetest dreams involved flight to other states and cities, anywhere but here.

Diaspora. They will take their language and their memories and customs with them, and they will remember their homes with fondness and nostalgia, as a place of innocence, a lost Eden. They will remember it as a simpler time. They will remember it as Arcadia, but they'll feel sorry for those who stay, as though they're failures.

At the Farm Progress Show, the corn grows higher and stranger, and they're finding leisure uses for soybeans: crayons and candles. You can buy nostalgic books and classic tractor calendars and yo-yos with the Dekalb flying corn logo, and you can buy towering machinery and hear lectures on the stock market, but you won't see a nonwhite face among the thousands of faces that you see. You will have to drive out into the fields where the tomatoes are being cut or packed, five miles away. You will have to get lost on your way to Windfall or Arcadia. You will have to drive to Hobbs.

The real Arcadia is a town filled with antique stores. It's a bus stop, a holding tank, a waiting station. You put your time in there, and you wait to die or leave. You can find it in an atlas of the world and go there if you'd like to see if this is true.

The factory itself was a large pole barn, around three stories high but open and light and filled with the sound of empty clinking silver cans. It was a lovely sound, like church bells or wind chimes. Up above my head the cans moved down cagelike chutes. They twirled and paused and dove in rapid constant motion from one side of the factory to the other. They swooped like birds. They were on a contraption very similar—in its slow climb and rapid fall and turns—to a roller coaster. I'm assuming in this simile that you've been to an amusement park. I'm assuming that you've never been to the tomato canning factory in Hobbs. I'm assuming you know that Arcadia is Eden, that Delphi is the home of wisdom, that Omega is the end of all. I'm assuming that you know all three are located just north of Indianapolis, in the American Middle West, at the end of the twentieth century. I'm assuming, in other words, that you're someone like myself. Because of that assumption, I can almost see you.

There were ten or so gloved men and women standing around a conveyor belt and sorting, one last human time, through tomatoes. In my memory I see them individually less clearly than I see you now, your eyes, this page. I see gloved hands picking rapidly over a moving belt of skinned fruit. I see the machinery. I see the silver cans. I think about how strange and new the landscape seems today. I think about how the October sun is stored in the flesh of the tomatoes. I think about the work of preservation in front of me, how important it will be to remember it, to be mindful in the cold, gray middle of the coming winter, of its undeserved and un-examined grace.

VENEER

Although specific rituals are necessary when the tree is cut down, carving the wood does not require special ceremonies.
—Diane Pelrine, curator, Art of Africa, Oceania, and the Americas, Indiana University Art Museum

I had come to the place that calls itself the veneer capital of the world. I was fishing for symbols. I expected to catch my limit quickly and head on someplace else. What else could you find in Edinburgh, Indiana, a place that sometimes forgets to include the silent "h" on even official documents, but irony.

I'd trained my eyes to look for certain things, and at first I saw them. The rusted cars, the complacent rural poverty, the way the road curves around the graphite-colored silos, the trashy railroad lines, the dust of dissolving brick on turn-of-the-century houses, the drooping shutters and cast-off kitchen appliances on porches, and the interminable gray skies. It was cold and windy.

The day before had been sunny and warm. You know there's only one other place on the face of the earth with weather as changeable as Indiana's, my son had told me. Ohio? I'd asked him. Illinois?

No, he'd said. Siberia. There are parts of Siberia, he said, where you'd swear you were home.

If there was a sister city for some gulag, I thought as I headed for the veneer factory, it would be Edinburgh. How could you live or work here? The ramshackle houses, the railroad tracks, the stacks of logs on trucks, in log yards, the aging factories on each side of town, each one larger than the town itself. And the sad little downtown with its attempt at beautification. Its one-way newly paved brick street with hardly any traffic, its two dollhouse-sized blocks with its hardware store and its bank and its boarded-up windows and its plastic flowers. Its veneer.

I was there a little early, so I stopped by the library to find what I could of local history. The library was new, paid for by a grant from the factory I was here to see. There were no locks on the restroom doors. Hey Ruthie, Mabel just went in there, you'll have to wait a minute. No stranger is likely to just drop in here off the highway, and we're all family, so who needs locks? You have to make a point to drive to Edinburgh. It's not on anyone's route to anything.

There was the usual display of self-help books, an ancient woman picking them up one by one to inspect them, like vegetables. I ask the librarian to point me to the local history. She looks surprised. Genealogy? She asks. No, history, I say. Genealogy, she says, and points me to another room.

Where all the books have similar names: *History of the Pruitt Family, History of the Stilabower Family, History of the Irwins.* This is where you come on those days when you want a literal answer to who you are and how and why you ended up here. You try to find a narrative arc in the family story, one that leads inevitably to your own, that makes it seem more drama than denouement, that gives it meaning.

Hidden within the genealogies there are those old beautifully illustrated nineteenth-century atlases and finally, what I'm looking for, a history of Edinburgh published by the sesquicentennial committee. Maybe I'll find an answer here. I want to know why, of all things, veneer? Why in this particular place? I think of veneer as a synonym for a kind of mask, for a falsification, a way to make something look expensive when it isn't. I think it must have been some industry that arose here by some accident or because of some entrepreneurial genius during the Depression, like Depression glass and movies and cosmetics, something to make you look better than you were actually feeling. I think of small towns in rural Indiana as at the very least being what they are and have been and what you expect them to be. That's why I'm expecting irony. What else could you find when you're studying veneer.

I look through the history and discover that there wasn't just one veneer factory, there were three. And that it had something to do with the railroad line passing through from Indianapolis to Louisville. Many midwestern towns were created, in fact, by railroads, as places to stop and pick up goods, usually grain or livestock or some natural resource. Like lumber.

When you drive down from Indianapolis to Edinburgh now, you see farmland and you see malls and subdivisions being built over farmland, but you don't see many trees. You grow up in the Midwest thinking that God put corn and soybeans outside of cities in some divine parquet pattern, that it's always been that way. You have to force yourself to reimagine that this was once one of the world's finest hardwood forests and that it went from being that to what it is now in less than one hundred years. So that explains the sawmills, and I'm supposing that a veneer industry developed as lumber became more scarce. That's my initial hypothesis.

Other than the mills, and the usual fires and floods, the other interesting thing in the history of Edinburgh is the effect of World War II, which blew in and out of Edinburgh as though there'd been a battle there. "Edinburgh," according to the history, "saw all its young men go to war. Not a single family was excepted." And of course Edinburgh rests on the northeastern edge of Camp Atterbury, the army base that was formed in fewer than ten days out of acres of farmland in June 1942. Families were moved off of farms; churches and homes and schools were blown up, the neighboring town of Kansas was obliterated, and the refugees found new homes in Edinburgh. The "girls worked in offices and women in the factories." The boys and men went off to Europe. Eighteen hundred new buildings were created in the army camp, including what was at that time one of the three largest army hospitals in the United States and housing for German and Italian prisoners of war. Where Kansas used to be, they built a false-front town nick-named Tojoburg, so soldiers could practice taking over a city and blowing it up. All this building required lumber.

The population of Edinburgh almost doubled in that year. People trying to get their sugar rations formed "crowds so thick in the general store that no one could move." Two years later, almost to the day, in 1944 the army base was closed. It opened again in 1950, during the Korean War, then closed again. The families that had been displaced and moved to Edinburgh were supposed to be allowed to buy their land back, but they never did. The sons and daughters of six-generation farm families became factory workers, and their sons and daughters became service providers and corporate bureaucrats. Most of them moved on to the larger engine factories in Columbus, and eventually their children moved away. In coming here, I was heading back into history.

According to the book, most people were heart-broken that the camp caused them to lose their homes. My husband's great-grandfather, who was from Kansas, committed suicide in 1947. He'd been forced to give up farming and had been working, I'll find out later, for a veneer factory in Edinburgh. "He must have hated," my husband's aunt told us, "working inside that mill."

I no longer expect to be amused. I just feel sadness when I walk outside the library and back into the town itself. All the things I'd noticed when I first drove in are what remains of sacrifice and a particular tragic history, of people who love a place long past reason.

It's a small, one-story office building, nothing much to look at from the outside, that universal aqua of small-town office buildings. But inside, the wood is, of course, beautiful—the paneling, the office furniture. Beautiful but not ostentatious, nothing like a city lawyer's office, say, or the lobby of a bank. It's simple and functional with polished wood and soft lights, but the lobby is small, like an elevator.

Let me introduce you, the receptionist says, to John Grunewald. A small man, elegant, with an accent that I don't recognize. I ask him why sawmills, here of all places, and two of them. This used to be some of the best quality timber in the world, he says. The best white oak was just south of Edinburgh and the best walnut was a few miles north.

It was the quality, he said. It has to do with the soil, the moisture, the temperature. All those things affect the wood grain. You can't force it.

So it's aesthetics. When you cut a quality log into strips for veneer, it seems, you multiply the opportunity for beauty. Each thin strip from that log has the qualities of the log's design, its fingerprint. Why not cover as much surface as you can with that design?

Where do they go now for logs? Iowa for walnut, he says. Maple from Michigan, Illinois for white oak, red oak from Ohio and Michigan, cherry from Pennsylvania. Now and then some older local timber will come up for sale, but there's not much of it.

What about Atterbury? I ask, thinking of all those untouched acres. It was mostly farmland, he says; it had already been deforested. And the timber that's left, he says, is full of bullet holes.

So logs are shipped here to be cut and then they're shipped out someplace else. One of our largest customers, he says, is a Korean piano manufacturer. They sell veneers in Korea, Malaysia, Singapore, China. Business in China is particularly good.

They're relatively new to this economic meltdown, Mr. Grunewald tells me. Indonesia is badly affected, and Thailand. Japan is a basket case, he says.

That paneling behind your desk, I ask Mr. Grunewald, is what? Brazilian rosewood, it was one of our specialties years ago. It's a rich red patina with drips of polished yellow. An exotic species, in the language of log buyers. Guitar veneer. Rain-forest wood, several decades old.

He tells me that the yellow strip is sap. Maple is all sap, he says, that's why it's so light. That color in light-colored furniture is bleach or sugar. The desk? I ask. Amboyna burl, from Burma. A burl? A cancerous growth, he says, the grain grows every which way, and it's extraordinarily beautiful.

The burl looks smokey and vaguely both starlike and amoebalike, similar to those new photos you see of galaxies that look so much like swirling blood and amniotic fluid. A burl. The desk legs are black ebony and are from Indonesia. They're both valuable and rare, like jewels.

I look around the office. The mask? Senegal, he says. The room is filled with paintings and sculptures. That one by the door? Pre-Columbian, he says.

And the accent?

Hungarian, he says. He's Hungarian.

How did he end up here in Edinburgh? Where did this artwork come from?

Jerome will show you around the factory, he says. And then come back here. I'll tell you.

Jerome is waiting in the outer office. He's wearing a leather coat. He smiles like John Travolta, that kind of smile. Poor thing, he has to walk this woman who thinks of veneer as nothing but an interesting metaphor through his plant, this woman who can tell metonymy from synecdoche but can't tell white oak from red. What good is she? There are four interns from different parts of Europe living in a farmhouse outside of Edinburgh, just to learn to judge a piece of wood, like wine. What will he do with me? He'll be charming and gracious and make this a quick tour.

It doesn't matter. I think of these processes like some language that at some point in future history we will have forgotten how to speak. I'll never know the language, but perhaps I can gesture toward the rich and complicated culture that arose from it.

A gray day, and there are logs with gray bark lying stacked in the log yard, and they're stacked by species— walnut, cherry, white and red oak, maple. They're graded before they come here, and then there are men who walk around the yard and grade them a second time. The lower-quality logs are marked with blue ink for export. There are mounded burls, like mushrooms.

The logs go into a machine outside the mill that removes the bark so they're white and shivering when they disappear into the sawmill. The bark goes into a mulch truck; all of the by-products are used for something else. I'm still thinking about World War II and watching the naked logs move along a chain.

There's so much violence in a mill.

You step inside and there is the screeching and thunder, the horrific sound, and steps that are too far apart made out of iron filigree rising up into the air, to a catwalk, and you walk up the steps and can always see what's going on right under you, and it's terrifying.

Two and a half million square feet a day, the pale logs are loaded on a machine that runs on rails, so when you're standing on the catwalk it's like looking down onto subway tracks, with that same rush of the train, only this time it's a log that rushes toward you on the tracks, with red laser beams pointing out where the log is to be cut and a sawyer sitting in a room above you. As if he were playing a video game, he points the laser and then there's the horrible sound of the blade squaring the log. It all happens so quickly, with so much sound and violence, and you're standing on the edge and right below you is this enormous blade and the wood and the tracks and you think of Anna Karenina and subway suicides and you just want out of there.

And outside the mill there's a pole barn filled with ovens, over here in this large warehouse, and it smells like vinegar and pitch. You look down into enormous stainless steel vats where the logs steam in their own juices, a blue-black tarry group, like dark swimming pools, twenty-six of them, kept at 190 degrees to heat the moisture that's there inside the log, to soften the wood, like warm butter, for slicing. Every kind of wood cooks for a specific length of time. And then someone planes the outside of the log to remove the dirt and grain.

The log is cleaned and heads into the knife blade. The log moves up and down and the blade remains stationary. It's sliced into sheets like a potato or an onion and each sheet is stacked in sequence then, like collating a book, because the thing about veneer is that you can match it, you can make a pattern, like with tile or wallpaper, or a clone.

There's a woman whose entire job is to flip each sheet individually onto a dryer that sucks it up against itself and then drops it down on the other side, where there are two more women who stack them once again in order. Everything is stacked into sheets and then checked, like tobacco leaves. They pull a sheet from the top, the middle, and the bottom and grade them once again. Like tobacco, the price will be different between one log and another. The buyers come here and they haggle, like they're at a market. There's a part of this manufacturing that can't be controlled, the design that appeared over years of growth, and that means the price will vary.

The slices of veneer are soft and pliant, like a fish.

When the veneer is dry and flat, it's stacked in a warehouse in containers like giant flower presses. And then it's sold. And some is shipped to companies you'd recognize from *The Price Is Right*—Broyhill and Thomasville and Drexel. And some is exported. The ratio is about 50:50, Jerome tells me. The other Edinburgh mill is primarily export now. And so it goes.

Come have lunch, Mr. Grunewald says, and I say
that no, I really couldn't. You have to eat, he says, it will
save you time on the way back. I have to pick my son
up from school at 3:00, but there's probably enough
time to eat lunch, so I thank him and we head past office cubicles and down a hallway.

Edinburgh, Indiana, with its brooding church and
graveyard on the highest point, is a town so small there
isn't even a fast-food strip or Subway sandwich shop, so
he takes me to a modest lunchroom, maybe eight small
tables without cloths, and we stand in a short line for
food. There's no place to eat in Edinburgh, he says, so
there are local women who cook and bring the lunch
each day. He asks if I'd like a glass of wine with lunch,
or beer. He asks other people in the line around him,
and they decline, not today, but thank you. I love the
outgoing president asking secretaries and salesmen and
women and clerks if he can serve them. The food is rare
prime rib with several kinds of sauce and vegetables and
homemade rolls and tea and freshly made lemonade.

We sit next to a Chinese woman who's in charge of
sales to China. He offers us an espresso or a cappuccino.
She takes cappuccino and he walks across the room to
get it for her and for himself a triple espresso as thick as
Turkish coffee. How's it going now? he asks her. They're
on holiday this month, she says, but sales are good. This
is the year of the rabbit? he asks. Yes, she says, the
rabbit.

What do they do with American veneer in China? I ask, thinking of Chinese children my daughter's age playing Chinese instruments coated in exotic American oak, some kind of instrumental Chinese postmodern fusion, like Thai/Mexican/French cuisine or jazz/rock/Indian/Scottish highlands/country music.

They put it on musical instruments and furniture, she says, and they send it back here.

Say what?

They send it here, she says. The workforce is much cheaper, so the veneer is sent there to American companies hiring Chinese labor and then the furniture is sent back to the United States and to Europe.

Wouldn't it be cheaper to save the costs of shipping? And what about robots and automation? Wouldn't that be cheaper if labor costs are so high?

A furniture company can hire twenty people in China for less than one person here, she says. And it's cheaper to pay shipping and hire the human labor than it is to incur capital costs and buy expensive machinery.

They make the veneer here. They have the expertise and the natural resources. They could send whole logs, but it can cost as much as $4,000 to ship them. You're paying for a lot of excess when you ship a log—for the bark and corners. The furniture factories in the United States buy the best veneer for top-of-the-line furniture, but you pay a lot for the labor. The American companies in China buy the lower quality veneer, manufacture the furniture cheaply, and ship it back to us. It remains lower-end furniture.

In one case the veneer is more of a cosmetic. In another, it's an element of design, like paint. It depends on the skill of the manufacturer. It depends on what's hidden underneath the surface and how well the furniture's constructed.

There are mall export stores that sell relatively inexpensive cherry-veneered furniture. You know the stores, the ones that play on the language of British colonialism, a language of power and wealth, of imperialism. You're buying a historical allusion to something exotic and foreign and expensive, filled with mosquito netting and butterflies. It's an allusion that hides another history, of violence and misunderstanding, and the inability to see whole groups of other human beings as real. You're paying, in this case, for a mask. You're paying for veneer. In both the history alluded to, and the present one, the veneer is hiding similar truths.

It's a face mask made by the Dan people from the Côte d'Ivoire. It's made of wood and pigment, iron, copper, monkey fur and felt, of cotton thread. The monkey fur is used for a giant mustache and beard under a straight-edge nose and Modigliani eyes. The wearer of the mask "sheds his human nature" and speaks with a spirit voice, with that authority. "The Dan believe," according to Diane Pelrine, "that all masqueraders are the physical manifestations of spirits who live in the forest and were its original owners."

The craftsman who carved the mask saw the spirit first in a dream. Incarnate me, the spirit says, and the craftsman does as he is told. He builds the mask around the spirit. The wood and fur and felt and copper are formed around him, pressed like clay; the artist can feel the spirit in his hands in the same way, I imagine, a mime finds the wall or object in space as though it's something solid that he's come upon. The materials are pressed like stickers on a suitcase, like that, and it's an outward, visible sign of something holy, that work of art, and it's worshiped with offerings of blood and egg and kola nut, and there's still that patina of offering on the wood.

Where did this artwork come from? He whirls a hidden compartment in a burled maple wardrobe and takes a book from underneath some other objects, and he gives it to me, a gift. It's a catalog from a show at a museum: *African Art from the Rita and John Grunewald Collection.*

We were on the trade route, he says, quite by accident. Decades ago, sellers brought these works to motel rooms in Bloomington. He was attracted, he supposed, to the use of wood. In Europe, veneer was accepted earlier in the nineteenth century because there it was a craftsman's art. "It wasn't a question of cost," he said, "it was a question of design, of beauty. If there's a good match, or if there's a pattern, it's usually veneer."

In the United States, veneer had more to do with practicality. It was mass produced, a way of conserving resources, not at first for conservation's sake, but for maximizing profits. That's why it has that bad name.

Grunewald is from Hungary, from a family of fine wood craftsmen. His uncle, I'll read later, was the finest veneer craftsman in Europe when World War II broke out.

Grunewald majored in philosophy and art history in college. Is the aesthetic experience of grading wood similar to that of collecting art? I ask. I'm trying to get at something but am not sure what it is quite.

Maybe it's some spirit, some dream I'm having here in the veneer capital. It's not the same, he says. And how is it different? One is an artistic idea, he says, and the other a question of discovering a pattern. Is it meaning? I ask, and he says, No, that art doesn't always have meaning either. One is man-made and the other nature-made, he says. Man doesn't influence the looks of the wood. What man can do is to open the log in a certain way to discover what is there. You can't tell before you open it, and you have to open it correctly, he says. It's like cutting diamonds. You have to do it right. Some logs, no matter how you open them, there's nothing there.

Where were you when World War II started? I ask him, still thinking of the army camp outside of town, of the displaced farmers. I was a child, he said. I was sitting in a restaurant in France, having breakfast.

I looked up, he said, and I saw the waitress crying. And then my mother was crying. I asked my mother, Why are you crying? We were vacationing in Normandy.

We went back to Hungary but couldn't return through Germany.

And what did you do then?

Just tried to survive, he said. Just worked to survive.

His uncle was a lucky one and was able to come to the United States. Grunewald's family was Jewish.

John Grunewald was still a boy when the war was over. He was fourteen years old. My uncle, he said, sent a smuggler to Hungary to get me. It was very difficult to get out from behind the iron curtain, but here I am, he said. In Edinburgh, Indiana.

I don't ask him what happened to him during the war. I know the history of Hungary. Up until 1944, the Hungarian government protected the Jews. In that year Eichmann tried to barter Jews for money and goods from the Allies. At one point he offered 350,000 Jews for 2,000 trucks. The Allies refused. So Eichmann deported all 350,000 of Hungary's Jews to Auschwitz. Two hundred fifty thousand of them were gassed within two months.

His uncle brought him to the United States, sent him to good schools. One decision leads to another. He ended up running a veneer mill in Edinburgh, far away from Hungary. He says everything with sincerity, as though each moment is filled with equal parts pain and sweetness.

Does he think about philosophy as he works? No, he says, I think about where I'm going to find logs, what I'm going to say to politicians the next time I travel to Washington.

Who were your favorite philosophers? I ask, and he says, Bertrand Russell and Bergson. This place is mysterious and beautiful and strange and civilized in a way that's much deeper than veneer, as mysterious and beautiful and strange as virgin forest, as human survival, as the ability, after everything, to love anything that man has made. Every place is so filled with human history that you could study it your entire life and never get to the bottom of its sadness.

INDUSTRIAL GOTH NIGHT
AT THE MELODY INN

Music must represent the spirit of crowds, of great industrial complexes, of trains, of ocean liners, of battle fleets, of automobiles and airplanes. It must add to the great central themes of the musical poem the domain of the machine and the victorious realm of electricity.

—Balilla Pratella,
Technical Manifesto of Futurist Music, 1911

Liberated from the tyranny of the pavement, you'll move across the surface of your world with a confidence you never dreamed possible.
—advertisement for the H2 Hummer, 2000

The Melody Inn is an old bar, dark and moody and supremely out of fashion. It sits on Illinois Street near a plasma bank, right between a pawnshop and a costume store. The mannequins in the costume store are always dressed for the season, but it's April and April is not a particularly costumeable month. It's the slow time after

Easter and before Memorial Day. So the mannequins are dressed in togas in the hope of orgies.

The Mel is the only bar on this street, and there are no restaurants or clubs. There's a grocery store that closes at 5:00 on Sunday nights, a hardware store that's been closed all day, and a playground without any children.

My friend Barb and I get a parking spot on the curb right in front of the bar.

Before we left home, our teenage children said we'd look like freaks in our mother costumes. It's in our nature not to care, of course—or to tell our kids we don't. We're at that stage in life. Barb was so sick of obsessing about her hair that she cut it all off and everyone thought she'd gone on chemotherapy. Other than that, we're fairly non-descript and happy about it. If asked, we'd both say we hated fashion. Though we're dressed, I'm sure, in our own way, as predictably as the mannequins.

They say that there are marketing people who could drive by any house and tell you what's in a person's closet, who could take Barb's hair and cross it with the car she drives—a white Jeep Cherokee—and tell you what brand of dish soap she buys; who could take my Nissan and cross it with my black long-sleeve tee and predict the content of my pantry. You're probably be-ginning to do that yourself from the hints I've given. These marketing teams, wherever they are, have already predicted where I'll want to live and what I'll want to wear and eat and drive when I retire. They know what I'll buy my grandchildren for their sixteenth birthdays. They know what kind of funeral I'll want, and where I'll want to be buried. Why waste all this time making decisions? I've never been very good at them anyway.

But which one of those marketing geniuses could predict that Barb and I would want to go to Industrial Goth Night at the Melody Inn late in April in the first year of a new century. We've foiled them. We're outside the box and feeling giddy.

I wouldn't mess around with that goth stuff, my son says as I leave, as though he were the parent and I his child. It's research, I tell him, for this book on factories. Why gothic with industrial? Why not rational and industrial or gothic and romantic. Once I understand it, I say to him, I'll come back home and behave more predictably.

What did I expect? I pictured kids with white painted faces and Elvira hair and vampire teeth. Sweet, fragile girls lost in episodes of *Buffy*. At some level I knew that Barb and I would be the out-of-context freaks like that Eudora Welty story where the women in the beauty parlor talk about a sideshow while the permanent wave solution drips onto their necks and their hair is wired with metal or plastic rollers and the face powder settles into the damp folds of their skin. I was sick of feeling like a mother. Please don't sing along with that. Whatever you do, don't dance.

Of course, we got there way too early. There was nothing to see. The windows were covered over with black plastic tarpaulins, and the mirror behind the bar was smudged with smoke and fingerprints and there was the obligatory pool table with the four obligatory boys who now and then lifted the table's edge and dropped it on the floor like thunder.

Barb and I sat near the back. The boys looked like any college boys. There were two tables with quiet heterosexual couples, the boys wearing black plastic Buddy Holly glasses and the girls with short cropped hair and black T-shirts, not much there to remark on finally. Nothing goth or particularly industrial.

At ten after nine a young woman breezed in the bar and collected the cover charge from the ten or so of us who sat there, and then the music started and the lights came on: primary crayon–colored lights on the tips of a bouquet of bendable black tubes. The lights swirled and dipped around the stage, and the girl began to dance. She wore a long black leather coat and under that a long-sleeved minidress, brown and painted with some black hieroglyphics resembling spiders' webs or skeletons. The tube lights and another white light, a strobe, made her movements seem fragmented, related to the fluid motion of ballet as, say, the steering wheel–sized red pillow dots of a George Wilson/Herman Miller marshmallow sofa is related to a more traditional sofa, as though it has exploded into its separate particles, each one surrounded by air.

Now and then the music sounds like factory noise. This is postindustrial music inspired by industrial noise. Oddly nostalgic. Oddly religious, an homage to some dying god. Factories are the cathedrals of capitalism, the real cathedrals—more overwhelming than the malls, more awe-inspiring, less on a human scale. There are no melodies in this cathedral. The music is atonal.

I'd love to be up there doing that, Barb says, and your heart aches. Why not? We could get up onto the stage and dance, we agree. There's no one here but a bartender and two couples and four college kids playing pool and one industrial gothic dancer. No one would ever know. We wouldn't tell our children. They can't even stand to see us dance to the radio in our own living rooms. Children are tyrants, but we forgive them because we were, in our own time, tyrants as well.

But here, we could let go, we could whirl and dance in our mother costumes, but we won't. Somehow this young girl, a little older than our children, this girl who had the courage to talk the owner into letting her do this on a Sunday night and the entrepreneurial energy to advertise it in the Sunday paper and then whatever it takes to dance like this all by herself on the stage with the sound man playing the disks and the light man starting the smoke machine and arranging the multicolored lights when no one, clearly, is coming to her party, is a stand-in for our daughters. If we were to get up there with her and dance, we would be breaking an unspoken agreement we've made with all girls their age, that this is their time to dance under the lights. We've taken the urge to dance like this and pushed it into the smallest space that it could occupy and now and then it burns and now and then we find ourselves choking on it but mostly we know that it's a sacrifice, a stepping back, a winding tight of some cosmic spring for that humming jewel-like engine underneath our daughters' feet, the one with tiny metal teeth like a thumb piano that keeps them bobbing up and down so beautifully and with such ecstasy.

Barb and I stay and watch the girl dance and talk with her sound man and the bartender for about an hour. The girl smiles and thanks us as we leave, as though we're some long-lost relatives.

Outside, the block is blank and empty, like un-stamped metal. There's a red glow on the windshields from the neon letters in the window of the Mel. The pawnshop has a new selection of banjos and guitars. Someone's left a light on in the dry cleaners. There's a Singer sewing machine in the window, glossy as a black widow spider, entangled in its spools of multicolored threads. The wigs in the wig shop across the street are Kool-aid colored: lime green, blue raspberry, and cherry. The windows of the plasma bank are shaded with white paper. The mannequins are a Greek chorus. What are they saying? Barb and I are the only mortals on the street, and our ears are ringing and we feel too old to hear them.

So why, I ask, as we drive off, were there so few people there?

Barb laughs and says that we probably left before it really started. And besides, she says, what goth girl would know to advertise in the Let's Go section of the Sunday paper? Where people like her mother, like us, would read it and say, Hey let's go to industrial goth night. It could only be a goth girl who's suburban.

I imagine most midwestern goth girls are suburban, I say. It takes a lot of upkeep. You have to watch *Buffy* and have a computer to access the Web sites, and you have to buy a lot of makeup.

And anyway, Barb says, this is retro-goth, about a half decade past its prime.

How did she ever talk the guy who owned that bar into letting her run her own dance party on Sunday nights? How did she think of it? Why the Mel of all places? I say. I wonder what she'll be doing ten years from now.

She'll run a dot.com, Barb says. She'll be married, have some kids.

And when she's made enough money that she can afford a too-expensive car, I ask, and when she needs one large enough to cart those kids and their friends to sports and lessons, what will the market experts say she'll buy? Definitely not a minivan, I say. She might as well slit her wrists.

And not an SUV, Barb says.

Maybe a big old Cadillac or station wagon, something retro-fifties, like her grandparents drove, I say. That's always safe.

Or monorails or bicycles or those cunning little butterfly-looking papery solar things.

What will a maturing industrial goth girl want to buy?

She's dancing out of fear, Barb says, and not nostalgia. In ten years that girl will want to drive her precious babies in a tank.

Some corporation had to know, or think it knew, the answer to this question. I liked this tiny dancer. I wanted to know how the table was being set for her future, and by whom. I like to think that she'll subvert whatever conclusions have been drawn, that she will be the creator of her own environment, and not passive, that she'll build a house that looks like a shell if she wants to, all filled with whorls of blue and green and red see-through glass bricks, that she will freely choose her own garden shears and her own adult broom and that she will commit herself to things she chooses and hold on to them through changes in fashion and color waves and so resist filling landfills in someone else's backyard with all her cast-off perfectly good sofas even if the one she bought at twenty-five in a fit of passion makes her feel, at thirty-five, old and cast-off herself. Still, I wanted to find out what the powers-that-be thought she would drive her children in.

As it turns out, Barb was right.

The think tank at General Motors has come to the conclusion that the kids who reach adulthood in the 1990s will want to drive a car, when they reach their affluent years, that looks military, that can go on all terrains if need be, even if the most likely terrain they'll drive on will be streets from one urban parking lot to another. When asked to name a brand they thought would be the coolest, they said a Hummer.

So GM contracted with AM General, the makers of the military Hummer and the rich person's toy—the H2 Hummer—to make a third-generation truck called the H2 just for Gen Xers. "It's a call to more people to experience what Hummer is—the lifestyle, the philosophy, the confident attitude," according to the advertising. It will be several inches narrower but will retain "Hummer's image of strength and brute force." AM General will make it. GM will market it. In order to fill the market, the Hummer plant in Mishawaka, Indiana, is buying two miles' worth of private homes and razing them for a new factory. They're going to make urban military assault vehicles. They're expecting kids like my goth girl to buy them when they're in their thirties.

In this postindustrial, post–cold war age, we want to sit on Eames industrial-inspired chairs completely and purposefully devoid of any ornamentation or reference to the organic world and to drive military vehicles we saw dropping from helicopters into Bosnia and Kuwait. Why?

Of course we've never experienced a war at home, and so there's that romantic nondomestic edge that all things military have. Exotic. Dionysian. Blow up this pleasant dull street with all its sleepwalkers and let me run my heroic ego wherever the hell I please in this brief time I'm allotted. Who hasn't felt it? That dangerous exhilarating feeling. One of the most amazing passages in German poetry was written by Georg Heym at the beginning of the twentieth century, in 1910, another time when everything industrial and military was glorified. "It is always the same round," he wrote, "so dull, dull, dull. Nothing happens, nothing, nothing. If only for once something would happen and not leave behind this stale taste of triviality. If only barricades were set up again, I would be the first to take my stand on them. Just to feel the intoxicating enthusiasm, I would welcome a bullet in the heart. Or if a war could just be started up, however unjust a war. This peace is so damned oily and greasy, like a sticky polish on old furniture."

But why else? In a world in which she feels powerless and manipulated, increasingly anonymous, it will give her a sense of power. Or maybe it's not a symbol of anything at all. Maybe it's just the swing of fashion. It's not her mother's minivan in the same way that her mother's minivan was not her grandmother's station wagon or her great-great-great-grandmother's Conestoga. The function remains consistent. You need something to cart around the dishes and the kids and the occasional crab apple tree. That much doesn't change. It's only the changing form that makes you feel as though the world has never seen your kind before. So you'll never grow old and stop dancing like those other generations.

U.S. 20 bends and curves because it follows the St. Joseph River into Mishawaka. For a good while you drive by u-pick strawberry patches and river homes on stilts and stands of sycamore and birch and so the Hummer factory takes you by surprise. Acres of Hummers, mostly camou-green right now, but a few desert tan. As my guide will tell me later, when you drive a Hummer, heads turn. So imagine acres of them. When my children see one parked in a lot, we have to stop going wherever it was we were going and drive right back and get out and walk around the thing. It's an amazing object, squat and rectangular and extraordinarily cool.

The Hummer is the ultimate functional object, like a chair that's nothing more than a piece of curved plastic on metal legs. It's short and boxy so it won't tip over—only seventy-two inches high—but the drive train is sixteen inches off the ground so you can go over boulders or drive through three feet of water. And you can see the rivets in the construction. It calls attention to its human fabrication. It's rationally designed. There's nothing about it that might occur in nature, like a flower or a blade of grass or wing or claw. The camouflage colors are only so it can hide within the natural world, but its best setting might be asphalt- or mall-colored or the color of a computer monitor.

As the guard lets me in the gate, I drive by rows and rows of them and think that if it's cooler than a Jeep, and it is, it's partly in the low stalking animal look of it, but it's mostly in that windshield, wide but narrow like narrow sunglasses, like the kind of glasses you wear when you're so cool that your eyes are always half-shut with I've-seen-it-all-before cynicism. Heavily defended worldly eyes. That kind of cool. The parking lots of the Hummer factory are nothing more than acres of High-Mobility Multipurpose Wheeled Vehicles lying on the beach in shades. Waiting to be slung from a CH-47 Chinook or a UH-60A Blackhawk into the middle of some battle for truth and justice so that some kid who believes the lie can drive around in it and rotate a very real gun in the turret built into the roof.

If I sound bitter, it's because my son just turned seventeen, and the government has started sending him those lovely brochures about joining the armed forces, and I'd like for them to please stop trying to take my son away from me. Right now. Today. Just quit it. Take us off your mailing list. There is no seventeen-year-old male living in my house. You hear me? OK, now, that's understood.

But if there were, say, and if I'd had a conversation with him the night before, just testing, and asked him what car he would buy if he had unlimited funds, which he doesn't, his answer might have been (and unfortunately was) a Hummer. We watched a video they'd sent me from the factory in preparation for this visit. Three hours of advertising, and he couldn't take his eyes off it. It was all action, with no plot and only one theme—you too could own this. We watched it climb mountains and move over crevices and boulders, through rivers and swamps, up stairs. It worked like one of those remote-control cars he had when he was younger, the kind that go into walls and flip over, then come back again, the kind that drive right over table legs or your parents' shoes. Mom, I want a Hummer, my son kept saying. Let's sell the house.

Which is what it would cost, I say. A civilian Hummer H1, the kind you could buy now off the Internet, starts at $106,000. The company allows employees to borrow one for a weekend—for a daughter's wedding, say, or a reunion—to purposefully make some "previously owned" Hummers that sell for a bit less. The new H2s will be available when he's out of college, I tell him. And they'll start at $40,000. Start thinking about a job, I say. I'll just join the army, he says, and I say, *Don't you dare.*

My guide's name is Al. It's a union shop, he says, and he's worked there for thirty-four years, so he's got enough seniority to show people around all day. There are a few guys who've driven over from the NASCAR races in Michigan hoping to see the factory, and they're waiting at the gate. They have to make an appointment to come back tomorrow, and they're thrilled. This is like a trip to Mecca.

The first thing Al does is take me for a ride in the H1 civilian Hummer. It comes in nine colors, and this one is cherry red. You can get a wagon, a four-door hardtop, a convertible, or a slant back that looks more like the Desert Storm version. From inside, the damn thing's huge. There's an enormous console between the passenger's and driver's seats, and the same amount of space between the two seats in the back. There's enough space for ten seats, but you don't want to feel cramped in a Hummer. You own the road.

He takes me out on the test track, a slanted circular racetrack, and he starts going fast behind a military Hummer that's being tested before being shipped out, and I can't find the seat belt. For a while that seems OK but then we start going faster, around corners, and I scramble to find the belt and strap myself in.

He comes to the bottom of a hill that goes straight up 60 degrees. Ready? he asks, and I say, Oh sure. I feel like I'm on a roller coaster. At the top he takes his foot off the brakes and the Hummer oozes down the steep slope like it was nothing.

They only make a few of these civilian Hummers a year. Arnold Schwarzenegger has seven of them, and Mike Tyson owns six. Ted Turner has one, and Dennis Rodman, and Roseanne Barr and Bo Jackson and the

owners of football teams and both of the racing Unsers—
Al Jr. and Al Sr. It was Arnold, in fact, who talked the
company into making a version that civilians could buy.
He wanted one bad. It fit his image, was the only car
that did. They built him a tan one in 1991, with leather
seats.

I'm happy for him, I say. It's that mix of civilian lux-
ury and weaponry that creeps me out. Now they make
them in pewter, white, yellow, red, woodland green, and
this metallic color called mesa dusk.

Later, I'll read the newsletter that goes out to civilian Hummer owners. Every page, in its description of a
vehicle, uses the words *aggressive, raw,* and *tough.* My favorite article, in fact, is about a man named Robert S.
Silvers who owns a Hummer and has installed night-
vision capacity. "Think *Predator,*" the article begins.
"Think *Silence of the Lambs,* the killer . . . wearing bulky
night-vision goggles, the goggles turning the pitch-black
nothingness into an eerie green 'somethingness' that allows the killer to see in the dark."

Silvers has a TI/Raytheon NightSight system in his
'97 Hummer wagon. It cost $10,000. "I didn't really
need it," he said. "I thought it would be fun to have.
People glow and you can see where their body temperature changes," he says. "Wildlife lights up in the woods.
You can see if someone is hiding in your bushes when
you drive home." He operates the camera with a joy-
stick. He can see human beings up to 800 feet away, and

he uses it just to drive through the city. Sometimes he tapes the green warmth of human bodies and transfers it through his VCR right onto the Web.

The civilian Hummer has two tanks for gas, one holds twenty-five gallons and one seventeen. The seats are leather, and there are miles of controls on the dashboard, each one with a rind of lime-colored neon green. The inside of the civilian Hummer has that new car smell. When we're done with the test drive (it takes up two parking spaces) he lets me in the military Hummer— just as new but without that smell. I always thought that new car smell came from being new, that it was a factory, nonhuman smell soon replaced by the smell of french fries and hair and human skin. I thought it was the natural smell of the engine and the drivetrain and whatever it is that solders the whole thing together, but I was wrong. A brand new military Humvee doesn't have that smell.

And it doesn't take a key to start it. There's a toggle switch on the dash. You don't want to lose your keys in the sand, Al says, and have to call your mother for the extra set.

The doors come off the military Humvee. You can just pop them off and store them in the rear. There are only two seats, and they're covered in military olive drab. The turret has a place for a tow missile or a .30- to .50-caliber machine gun.

He takes me through the factory where the vehicles are constructed. It's clean and spacious and well lit. On one side of the building there's a row of purple windows, and that grape-colored festive strip throws light on the gold-colored parts of the Hummer body that are stacked everywhere you look. They're the same color as C3PO in *Star Wars,* and it feels like that scene where he's taken apart and scattered.

There are barrels of exhaust pipes and engine parts. There are American and European mufflers and there are mufflers that go into the trucks that wind up in Israel, where they don't require catalytic converters. In fact, there are a lot of trucks on the line today that are heading for Israel. You can tell it, he says by the paint. Israel has this particular tan tone, he says, with a touch of gold.

There's a large pit running down the center of the floor with men and women standing in it; like those pits where you get the oil changed on your car. They're tightening bolts and checking drivetrains. They've humanized the pit with bumper stickers. *Death Is Coming,* one reads. *Violent Tendencies.* Another sticker advertises Red Wing shoes. Several warn of the approaching wings of Jesus. Several give the number of sightings of POWs or UFOs.

This is the only factory that makes this vehicle. There are five hundred suppliers of parts, 98 percent of them American-made, 2 percent from Venezuela. They sell the cars, they say, to any friendly foreign country that wants to buy one.

Now you'll see the robots, he says. We walk past driveshaft parts that look like honey dippers, past swirls of copper tubing for brake fluids, back to where the robot arms paint the chassis with camouflage. The paint area has a sign like the entrance to a town. *Bondoville,* it says. It is, Al says, the supervisor's name.

A human male with perfect black hair sits in a windowed room and controls the robot arms. The robots spray the bodies with paint. At first I thought the man was a robot as well, one of those talking Disney presidents, but then he turned and smiled at me.

Across the aisle there's a tall space that looks like a theater where another human being gets into some of the crevices a robot still can't reach. The human stands on a scissors jack that lifts him up and down, and he's dressed in the most incredible silver gray space suit. The theater he's standing in is a deep midnight blue, and he levitates as he sprays the engines. The wall behind him is covered by a waterfall, like one of those walls in the atriums of hotels. The waterfall traps the fumes and takes them to a holding tank in the basement of the building.

Basements of factories are often holding tanks. There's a basement of a factory near my home that contains a forceful natural springs. When they started to build the building, they discovered the springs but didn't want to change their plans. So they build a reinforced cement room to contain it and put in several pumps. Like the Hummer itself, factories rationalize anything nature puts in the way—springs or rocks or rivers or hills or human bodies.

And now the marriage fixture, Al says, and he takes me to a raised platform where the front, center, and rear sections of the body are joined together as one, he says, like man and wife. All three parts are that lovely gold Alodyne. There's a stack of rear fenders on their sides, and they look like gorgeous sleds.

The marriage is held together with something like Superglue and 2,800 rivets. It takes at least that much.

After the wedding, they go to war. Some are bulletproof, some not. It depends on this and that. With their movie star shades and circus tricks and newlywed status, the camera loves them. The Hummer first saw combat in Panama in 1989. It became a superstar in Kuwait. "My kids thought it was just great," one woman said, "that their mother made a vehicle that was in a war."

The sound of noise is the sound of machines. Centuries of quiet, individual sounds went by—compare the hush of a needle in a piece of cloth to the din of an entire room filled with electric machines grinding, each machine and so each series of sounds responding to the demands of the assembly line or of the human operator, of the function of the piece that's being made and not the way the sound will mesh with the sound next to it. Stand in the middle of a wood and it's hard not to start hearing patterns—scanning the bird calls (iambic, iambic, trochee), hearing pitch, the call and response of squirrels, the rise and fall of the wind through clattery green, the silences and then new conversations between different creatures—this one allegro, this legato, this in four-four time and this in three, everything existing in response to something else. If you listen for it you can sometimes hear that wonderful flying change from one time signature to another, like jazz. This is, of course, the romantic view that modernism tried to rebel against. That sentiment. Harmony.

In the Hummer factory I listened for and sometimes heard the intervals of pitch—a perfect third in that siren or in the hammering of those two machines. And there was rhythm, always even, but as in every factory it's completely unrelated to feeling unless it's put on a loop of tape and removed from this context then placed within the frame of human feeling in music you can move to. Every sound, in the proper frame, calls forth a response in the human body.

And the feeling when the sounds are taken outside the factory and placed inside the frame of the Melody Inn on a Sunday night in Indianapolis and danced to? Oddly enough, it's ecstasy. "The pleasure of noise," writes critic Simon Reynolds, "lies in the fact that it obliterates meaning and identity." Ecstasy. Such an odd thing. Not the same as happiness, quite. It's sexual. At times religious.

At the beginning of the twentieth century, in that blissful ecstatic time, noise was political. It was supposed to triumph over romantic sensibilities, to bring us into our true human state—unsentimental, unblinking. In the old music there was always the message that any sadness or tragedy in the universe could be resolved into harmony. Noise groups say to hell with that sweet romantic harmony of our parents, those napkins at the table, those church services, those carpeted stairs, and absurd clothing. Industrial noise groups wrote about extreme states: trauma, atrocities, possession. There was a desire for authenticity in a time when everything feels prepackaged. What we want more than anything is something that feels real. Something outside the subjectivity of this confining self.

The industrial music Web sites always mention Celine, Surrealism, William Burroughs, Dada, Michel Foucault, Samuel Beckett, the Marquis de Sade, John Cage. Industrial gothic Web sites also mention vampires. If the thrill of the gothic is in the secrets, the transgressive sex, and violence born of isolation and Victorian morality, and left behind in castles and moors after their true function, their true time in history, has passed, perhaps industrial gothic finds that same thrill in the impersonality of the postindustrial, in the unacknowledged evil that still lurks behind in corners of abandoned warehouses like the cobwebs because it was closed-off and hidden, like the benzene and lead left behind in urban soil. The sexual thrill of the bite on the neck. That demonic thrill.

"Our media has become nothing but a pawn of big corporations," one Web site states. "My generation was already mentally crippled when we had only 5 or 6 channels on TV and now we have up to 500." One authentic response to this becomes the scream.

When my daughter was in grade school, we discovered this trick. She would put her face up close to mine and hum a tone deep down in her throat and wait for me to find the same tone. When we locked into the hum, we'd increase the volume until it seemed to enclose us completely in this sphere of somehow oddly nonvibrating sound. It's like our voices became the same voice; there was nothing else outside of this one tone.

We tried the hum with other voices, but it didn't work. She tried it with her friends; I tried it with my husband. Other female voices came the closest, but there were no other voices in the world that would create this particular enclosing synergy.

When she answers the phone now, people mistake her voice for mine. This is often true, it seems, of daughter's voices. It has something to do with vocal cords that create sounds that are explainable mathematically—the stretch, the stop, the vibration. You can explain pitch by the length of a vibrating string. You can explain harmony mathematically, by the division of the strings in half and then half again. Our vocal cords are so similar that our voices vibrate in the air along the same resonant pathways, but if I start to sing with my daughter now, she says, Please don't sing that song with me. It breaks my heart. Corporations count on that swing, on our fear of being like our parents in their uncool, unfortunate costumes of aging flesh.

If my goth girl buys a Hummer to cart her babies in because her parents never would, so be it. The way war planes from the nearby air force base practice maneuvers over our house some summer days and seem to break through the sky like fiery angels, the way her dancing softens the sound of the machines, perhaps it will domesticate the symbol.

I have to have faith that's all it means. The universe itself is made of strings, the planets rise and fall on paths of them in ways I'll never understand. Spectrographic lines of light from distant galaxies look exactly like piano keys. Let's hope that we're hardwired for harmony.

UTILITIES

*A tool, device, or other implement used as an
adjunct to a more important machine. Exists in
reference to a machine as a dictionary exists in
reference to a poem. Designed for usefulness often
at the expense of beauty.*

And so, what is that hulking monstrous postapocalyptic building? Towering, black, with squidlike chutes
that spread around the perimeter. It's a building out of
scale with everything around it; it's out of tone. And
when you're walking from Nordstrom's to Planet Holly-
wood or you're watching a small white baseball float
into the evening ether, you wonder what the building is,
and you ask someone and no one has an answer to your
question, no one knows what it's there for, no one can
tell you why it hasn't been destroyed.

When you really stop to look at it, it's larger than the
mall, it's larger than the new hotels. It's ugly and enormous and weirdly invisible. A remnant of something, its

days are no doubt numbered. It can't be necessary. It should be someplace else, where we can't see it.

No one makes things anymore. It's a well-known fact. We all know things like this fact, and that brings us money, which is infinite and surreal and as green as a pop bottle. We use the money to buy the things that no one makes, and we don't wonder where they came from or how they're made. The things we buy are easily expendable. We live in a perpetual twilight.

So burn it down or blot it out, that dinosaur, blast it off the earth, whatever it is, we just don't need it.

I have to go just once inside another aging building. Because it's both enormous and invisible. Because all my life I've looked for something that could shake the foundations, something that could shake the stem and roots of my hair.

Coke

The solid product resulting from the destructive distillation of coal in an oven or closed chamber or by imperfect combustion, consisting primarily of carbon.
—Webster's New International Dictionary

The coke plant covers several city blocks. You can see the city from the coke plant because the city travels skyward, but you can't see the coke plant from the city because, for the most part, the coke plant travels closer to the ground. It's more likely to make you feel the rush of awe than any skyscraper. Skyscrapers are clean and sharp and rational. A skyscraper feels like order. The coke plant is dirtier; it spreads over blocks and spews hot steam. There are unexpected, mammoth shapes—triangular smoking towers and enormous silos. The purpose of the coke plant is the creation of impossible heat and the attempt to cool it down. Wherever you look, there are signs reminding you of dangers.

A section of Pleasant Creek runs through the plant. It's lined with discarded chunks of coal. The houses right outside the plant are dusty colored, shotgun, porches filled with discarded upholstered furniture. There are hookers a block away, and clots of people who are out of work. The coke plant spews its steam behind tall chain-link fences. It fills the horizon. You can't see it unless you drive here among the dispossessed. The coke plant feels like suppressed rage.

Inside, they superheat the coal to make the blocks of coke. They push the blocks into a quenching tower. Ten thousand gallons of water fall onto the hot, now steaming, coke. The flushing liquor cools the coke, and tar condenses out of it.

Out of tar, you make pitch and one hundred thousand other things including dye, vitamins, saccharine, explosives, and chartreuse sulphur.

Coke-oven gas is hydrogen and is just as flammable. At one time it was used to lift zeppelins. Coke is mostly carbon, and carbon is necessary in the production of cast iron. When you burn the coke to make iron, you gain both heat and carbon. The coke plant is powerful and efficient, as efficient as poetry.

To wit: the iron is used in automobiles that spin around on concrete ribbons and isolate the coke plant from the neighborhoods and businesses surrounding it. The coke is shipped to Honda and to Saturn and to General Motors. The coke-oven gas is pumped to the Power and Light to help produce the steam that heats the pharmaceutical company that makes your Prozac and heats the hospital where you go to repair your broken bones or, in rare cases, to replace your failing eye or heart or kidney with that of the car crash victim's. In all this process, they say that nothing much is lost.

You wear protective glasses and metal-toed shoes when you enter the plant. You pass by several guards. It covers several city blocks. It looms. When it was built a hundred years ago, it was out in the country. It's not intended to be pretty. When coke is exposed to air, it begins to consume itself.

Electricity

*One of the basic properties of the elementary
particles of matter giving rise to all electric and
magnetic forces and interactions.*
　　　　　—Webster's New International Dictionary

My home is home to two adults, two children, a guinea pig, a dog, and uncountable fish in glass aquariums lined with blue glass stones.

My home is also home to five televisions and many other corded objects made of black or grayish plastic: microwaves and clocks and stoves and VCRs and answering machines and modems and computers, many of them with digital red numbers, which usually track the time but which are, this morning, beating 12:00 exactly like a pulse because the electricity stopped, briefly, overnight.

Every single time I open the cabinet over my telephone, complicated manuals explaining how they can be reset tumble out at me, and I feel helpless.

When something electronic shuts down, I ask my son or daughter to fix it, and if that doesn't work, I dive into the sea of cars, and I take the object to the store where they will often say it's more expensive to fix it than to throw it out and buy a new one. So I throw it out. Last week it was a microwave, a month ago a printer. If the object is small enough, I put it in a trash bag and wait for it to disappear. If it's large enough, like an automobile, they'll let you trade it in and someone else will buy it and someone else and someone else, but eventually it too will disappear to the places these things go. Sometimes I'll put a larger object in a closet where it will sit, quite lifeless, with cords that tangle in coat hangers and get caught in boxes, and within a year or two the thing that looked so sleek at first will turn unaccountably and oddly quaint and heavy, but never charming enough to take out and put in the middle of a table with cut flowers and a bowl of fruit.

Power

Work done or energy transferred per unit of time.
See also, angels.

They suck it in through pipes and wires. They suck and suck and suck at it. The television sucks at it, and the computer. And the CD player and the clicking lamps and the miraculous dishwasher, and the coughing disposal and the trash compactor. While we sleep, the clocks and alarms and furnace slurp the wires like drinking straws, and when we're away from home they slurp at it, and when we wake up in the morning they take a big long gulp and turn it into hot brewed coffee, they turn it into air that warms the walls and rocks the curtains, they turn it into steaming water for our showers. They drink in power and light and do our bidding.

Indiana Gas

A subject possessing perfect molecular mobility
and the property of indefinite expansion.

The industries that located here included but were not limited to those that require extraordinary heat: iron, steel, and particularly glass. The county was known for glass: art glass, window glass, glass ball paperweights, glass lamps, and circular Ball dome jars and sealing lids for preserving summer where you could see and touch it on a shelf in your grandmother's basement.

It was the supply of natural gas that was, we believed, limitless, which is to say eternal. Gas burned in blue flambeaux on street corners; there were fountains of the flaming stuff. People kept the doors of their homes open wide all winter to let the heat escape. The gas was as vast as the distance to the stars, as blue in its burning as the atmosphere, the perpetual turning of a wheel on a perpetual decline. The gas burned, yet kept on rising. Miraculous. Circular. Four dollars a month for all the gas you could consume. It would be the source of power for the entire next century. We owned it all.

In 1902 the needles dropped on the gas gauges. In another year or two the gas was gone.

Steam

The mist formed when the gas or vapor from
boiling water condenses in the air.
—Webster's New International Dictionary

This is the building that produces the steam made from the coke oven gas. It produces heat. It produces warmth in winter: for the pharmaceutical company and the hospital, for National Starch and General Motors, for the university and the Hebrew National Kosher Food Processing; for homes and gas stations.

The landfill where my old microwave is sitting, where my old receipts and coffee grounds are mixed together, both buys and helps create the steam. Everyone buys it; it runs underneath the city in large pipes. The pipes are cleaned out regularly because this is not New York, and we mind the plumes; we don't want those things that remind us of the underground, the pipes and sewers.

To get inside, you climb a fire escape. You climb three stories.

Inside, the entire building shakes. The walls, the tables where you put your hands, the floor, it shakes and rumbles. Everything is covered with ash, and dark, and you're standing inside a large engine, a machine, inside the turn of the nineteenth century.

In the winter they can make a million pounds of steam an hour.

There are rooms filled with mills grinding the coal to the consistency of face powder. The pulverized coal mixed with air produces something like a gas that burns immediately, like dryer lint. The flash, the heat, the constant explosions. This is the second largest steam-producing plant in the country, second to New York City.

Outside the building: the baseballs, the families with their shopping bags, the stock markets, the virtual reality palaces, the computer screens in microbreweries. The football fans paint their faces blue.

Inside here where the heat is made, it's dark and loud and trembling, filled with pipes and boilers and things you're afraid to brush past because they might burn you. One hundred years ago men crawled into holes in the boilers. They would put in wood, light it, crawl back out, and throw in coal.

When the lights go out in here, they say, it's terrifying. No windows, all the noise and explosive heat and catwalks with drops of a hundred feet. Like Mammoth Cave without flares. You sit down where you are and wait for light to reappear.

Sanitation

*The application of measures to make
environmental conditions favorable to health.*
—Webster's New International Dictionary

Ash ponds, ash handlers, precipitators. The side of the building that faces the capital is kept cleaner than the back. The ash is removed dry, stored in silos, and dumped in an ash pond. A train hauls the ash away, five thousand tons of it, six or seven times a day.

Once there was a wedding at the Ramada Inn on the west. The bride, the groom, the wedding cake, all covered with ash.

Money

Any circulating medium of exchange.
            —Webster's New International Dictionary

What is it? Cotton and linen, it takes some craftsman seven years to learn to engrave it, longer than medical school. The production goes on all day long, all night. Intaglio. Seventy-three hundred sheets of bills per hour; printers hover over the machines, inspecting sheets of freshly minted bills. Bins of dark green ink like wet grass clippings. Ink spots, smears, discolorations, mutilated shredded bills sold in the gift shop, in the barrels of pens, wrapped around golf balls and jewelry, in plastic bags to take back home to your family—$100 from the U.S. mint. Take your picture by a stack of it; see what you're worth. The windows so old they're purple, the glassed-in printing presses. It's all here, on the other side of the window, so much money, stacks and stacks and stacks of it.

The new bills, why don't they look as green? Beige and simple, not as Victorian. I watch the money being made in July, and by October I hold the first new ones in my hand. Remember this? I ask my daughter. We took the bus to Washington, D.C., and watched it being made. The bus driver wore a tie printed with vintage buses. We saw the Capitol building and the monuments and all the busy, self-important people. They filled the subways, they ran from one station to the next in suits, and everyone looked busy and nervous, like people wearing uncomfortable, ill-fitting shoes.

For some reason, no one trusts these bills. At McDonald's, the drive-through woman holds it to the light to see some hidden blur. At Arby's, they mark it with a special pen. Deceptively simple to counterfeit, the man says, you can try to print your own at Kinko's. Bleach a dollar bill and print this new one on a color printer. But use this pen or hold it to the light, and you can see the holographic images float inside of it, this strange technology. Who needs the engraver, the strictly ornamental, the hidden messages in the elaborately coded text?

Nuclear Power

Energy that can be liberated by changes in the nucleus of an atom.
       —Webster's New International Dictionary

In 1955, Union Carbide built a 350,000-gallon swimming pool reactor to take to the Geneva Conference on

Peaceful Uses of Atomic Energy. Lying safely, we thought, beneath sixteen feet of water, the plates of uranium began slowly to disintegrate inside their aluminum boxes, making the surrounding water glow blue from the radiation. They switched the reactor off and let it cool a few weeks before lifting the reactor out and heading for Geneva.

There was a column in the Hagerstown, Indiana, paper about the laying of the cornerstone for the new nineteen-story building adjoining Radio City in New York to house the Crowell-Collier Publishing Company.

> That cornerstone was put into place by atomic energy rather than by human hands. . . . The two-ton cornerstone was lowered into position at the end of a chain attached to a motor atop a hoist, which was powered by energy produced by splitting ten U-235 atoms. A miniature reactor, an amplifier, and two relays were used. One relay was attached to the hoist motor and the other to a magnesium flare imbedded in a ceremonial ribbon stretched between the motor and the suspended cornerstone. A half gram of radium-beryllium was used as the neutronic source for bombarding the uranium-235. Each time a neutron struck one of the atoms, the latter was split, releasing 200,000,000 volts of energy. We heard a pronounced click as this energy, picked up by the amplifier, caused a gong to ring and a 100-watt fluorescent lamp to flash.
>
> This happened each time one of the ten atoms was split. After this the accumulated electrical impulse

was transmitted to the motor and the magnesium flare. The ribbon broke with a loud report and bright flash. The activated motor lowered the cornerstone into position.

Coal

A black or brownish black solid combustible mineral substance formed by the partial decomposition of vegetable matter without free access of air and under the influence of moisture and in many cases increased pressure and temperature, the substance being widely used as a natural fuel and containing carbon, hydrogen, oxygen, nitrogen, and sulfur as well as inorganic constituents that are left behind as ash after burning.
    —*Webster's New International Dictionary*

When the trains bring in the coal, there's a machine that lifts the car from off its bed. The car hovers over a large hole in the ground and then metal circles at each end turn it upside down. You can stand on the track and watch the coal fall into the pit: the roaring and clattering like a waterfall or, rather, like jars of pennies being dumped into a sorter or like sacks of marbles or gravel from a dump truck. Whatever you can bring to this image from your own experience, magnify it—the sound, the pit, the tons of coal.

The coal superheats the steam. The coke gas super-heats the steam. The water for the steam is piped in from the river.

And one thing more:

When things fall apart in this place, they fall apart quickly. Some of the mechanical boilers need adjustments every twenty minutes, and if the boilers fail, the buildings relying on the steam need to have it up and running within ten minutes. There are temperature and pressure gauges. There's fire.

And the thing you notice in this building is all the emptiness. The vast space, and the abandoned desks, some of them close to one hundred years old. In every room there's a dusty desk or two where someone used to sit, watching. Room after room, it goes on like this until you get to a single glassed-in room with one man sitting, peering out. In some rooms there's the green rectangle of a computer screen, a pair of aqua plastic gloves on a table, a calamine-colored, coal-dusted untouched desk.

At the very top of the building there's a room where three men sit on rotating chairs, surrounded by gauges and television screens. They sit high above the city, at the same level, say, as the governor who sits behind his own desk one street away. The men wear black baseball caps. One cap says *Protect Freedom.* On another there's a cross. Objects sit on top of their computer screens: a Mickey Mouse hat with a feather, a toy airplane, a walnut, a Santa Claus head, a boat, a plastic toilet, a radio station football by a snake. When things fall apart, these are the men who fix it. They punch at buttons. There are no women. On Christmas Day, there are sometimes only five men in the entire building. Where are the sons and daughters of the men who used to work here? What are they doing?

The three men type on keyboards. They make corrections. They sit back in their chairs. For much of the day, they stare at a television screen with what seems to be an unmoving image. You look at it yourself, and you see the slightest movement. It's a picture of the three smokestacks on the outside of the building, centered in the screen in black and white, a faint ribbon of the white exhaling from each one, just the faintest breath of smoke. Three smokestacks, the highest in the middle, the cross on the fireman's baseball cap. It's eerie because it's all in tones of gray and because it doesn't move and because it looks like Calvary. Why is the camera focused here? What or who is being sacrificed? Why is there such stillness? We watch, the fireman says. There are so many ways things go wrong in this life. And the statehouse is right across the street from us, and the stadiums, and the park. The senators get worried when the smoke gets thick. We make adjustments. This steam runs in pipes all through this city.

NOTHING OBVIOUS WAS
HAPPENING IN INDIANA

I walked out of the melt shop into the parking lot to
see what was happening in Indiana besides steel. It
was a cool Saturday morning, a few minutes before
sunrise. Nothing obvious was happening in Indiana.
—Richard Preston, *American Steel*

Somehow I get in a group of international MBA students from the University of Illinois. They emerge from
a bus made of steel, the words Fighting Illini painted on
the side.

It's a dream! It's a dream!

It's not a dream.

Everyone in my group is from Japan. They all wear
black business suits. I'm wearing old jeans and a sweatshirt and a hard hat and a green spark-proof jacket provided by the Director of Safety.

The MBA students assume I work here because I'm
dressed in industrial garb, and they ask me questions I can't
answer. I tell them I don't work here, but they continue to

ask me questions. Why is this mill here? Because Nucor Corporation likes to place plants "among farm people who were comfortable with machinery and hated labor unions," according to Richard Preston. And because Indiana was the center of the rust belt, and this mill would make steel out of busted-up junk—old cars and refrigerators and Fighting Illini buses.

This is where our economy attempts to resurrect itself, each bit of iron from the earth doing its part to create more wealth, over and over again. Decades worth of steel is brought here in railroad cars as chunks of trash and come out the other side all shiny and galvanized.

"We're going to leapfrog Japan," said Nucor's CEO, Kenneth Iverson, in 1987. So we leapfrogged them, and here they are seeing how we did it. Nucor is now the second largest steel company in the United States, and according to the plant controller, "We'll be the biggest shortly into the next century."

According to the instructional video I'd watched in the administration building, Nucor attributes its success to the lack of unions. New workers who see this video are told they won't lose time and money to strikes, that they have job security because they won't be replaced during strikes, that customers trust Nucor because they know their supply of steel won't be interrupted by—you guessed it—strikes. The enemy of American steel, according to this video, were the unions. This plant is located about an hour away from the birthplace of Eugene Debs.

A sign over the steel mill door says that this is the site of the *World's First Thin-Slab Caster*. It's a shabby sign. The mill's controller had tried to explain the caster to me in the office, how a thin-slab caster is different from a conventional one, how this mill is to the larger steel mills in Gary as a laptop is to an ancient mainframe—it does all the same things and more in a smaller space and more efficiently.

"Everything in here," the Director of Safety tells us, "you can assume is hot, so don't touch." Throughout the tour, one of the MBA students will touch everything she sees. I feel like the Director of Safety's assistant. I feel like I'm walking through a steel mill with my daughter. The student has on heels and a perfect black suit. Don't touch, please don't touch that, I want to say. And still she touches it. She seems to have an uncanny sense for knowing exactly what things aren't hot because she never once gets burned, though at one point she slips on mud.

She slips on mud because her slick-soled business shoes are designed for an office, not the inside of a factory. Her life is not preparing her for this kind of tour. For a moment I think about the British troops all dressed in their perfect red coats in the Revolutionary War and I feel particularly American. We've leapfrogged Japan, and its economy is in meltdown. No wonder: They wear business suits on a trip to a steel mill. I'm identifying with the steelworkers. I'm expecting to see many of them, all looking like Arnold Schwarzenegger.

Meltdown. I think of nuclear metaphors and war metaphors. I think of purses made out of old license plates and perfume made to smell like fresh plastic and nail polish colors with names like Acid Rain and Slag. I think of dance clubs decorated with metal beams, all that tough and hip industrial chic. I'm thinking of the postapocalyptic spaces my students who are into vampires or futuristic fantasy always paint in their stories. Where's the setting of this story? I ask them and they always say, you know, an abandoned factory. A meat-packing plant or car-manufacturing plant, something dusty and functional and evil and they love it and today so do I. They associate factories with the demonic and they associate the demonic with youthful swagger. Today I'm brash and practical and ready to do battle with hot metal. I've got on my hard shoes and my hard hat and I look like hell.

And it seems I've entered it.

Think of every image of hell you've ever seen—the steaming flames coming out of nowhere, the heat, the rivers of fire, and that's what you'll see here. Believe me, when I've gone into industrial spaces looking for something to be awed by, it's occurred to me more than once to wonder what kind of power it is I'm looking for. If it's hell, I've found its image in Crawfordsville, Indiana. It's beautiful and powerful and scarey. If I'd known what to expect, I might have dreaded it. But a trip through hell, if it's just a tour, is also a thrill. There's not much narrative tension in perfection.

You've seen the scenes in movies. An unsuspecting someone suddenly finds himself in a line of other unsuspecting someones, usually because of an eruption of catastrophe or violence where some freedom has been forcibly removed—a line of prisoners, in other words, or slaves or exiles—and he or she is forced into some architectural space designed to instill terror, awe, and submission. The structure is massively out of human scale, some building with a ceiling higher than God that says: You are an unimportant human being, or not quite human, held together by a fragile skin. You are a microscopic nothing made of water and carbon kept in some weird balance that keeps you from bursting into flame. This system is much more powerful than you will ever be. I am a king, I am a sorcerer, I am a witch, I am a dictator, I am a power from some distant planet, I am a god. This is the outward and visible sign of my infinite power. You will give yourself to me.

That's what it feels like when you enter a steel mill. It's elemental and huge and powerful. You feel fragile and small if you're not part of it. There are places in a steel-making furnace where the iron reaches 6,000 to 16,000 degrees, one and one-half times the surface temperature of the sun. There are days when a single mill requires as much energy from a state's power grid as an entire city.

The part of the mill that houses the casters that turn pure molten metal into red-hot slabs of steel is as large as the inside of the largest cathedral. It's like the inside of an atrium in a hotel where you can look up eight floors but instead of marble and glass and a see-through elevator there's the bare steel sheeting of the building and giant hooks hanging a hundred feet above your head. Now and then these giant hooks move from one end of the building to the other carrying big kettles of melted iron ore and carbon—hot liquid steel fresh from a furnace. You imagine it falling from the ceiling with you standing underneath it. You'd ignite. You'd be ash. Not even your bones would remain. And there are sirens screaming and the Director of Safety warns us to be careful because in a steel mill there are so many things that can kill you just like that, as though it's not obvious.

Massive architectural space can be designed to make you feel a part of some ecstatic process, a process that, depending on its effects and purposes, can be either creative or destructive, either Mussolini's arenas or a cathedral. In none of the factories I've visited has the power of industrial space been more obvious than in a steel mill. We walk through dwarfed by it, awed by it; and the students, who have been joking and smiling, begin instead watching where they put their feet, holding on more tightly to their important briefcases.

They belong in a city with other MBA students from all over the world, where they'll talk to each other through cell phones and computer networks and they'll make decisions fiber-optically that will make their corporations money that no one will ever see because it's all done electronically. Profits are never something you hold in your hand, never something that will burn you if you touch it. Money is powerful and invisible and fluid in its own way, but it's pure symbol; it exists because we have faith in it. Pour enough of it into Crawfordsville, Indiana, here at the end of nowhere, and you can build this dangerous cathedral where, only one hundred years ago, the rivers were ten feet deeper than they are now, where there used to be a forest so dense it blocked out the sun. The problem with a virgin forest is that it feeds on decay, on the eater and the eaten. It's difficult to maneuver through, and it's terribly isolating, and the beauty of the crystal water and the sycamores as thick as trucks and the hummingbirds and soil as rich as kindling isn't enough to keep you from thinking about the danger in each step or about the fragility of bodies, the way they liquify so quickly into nothing. The purpose of this place is to allow us to leave that and forget it. What's manufactured here is a material stronger than human flesh. We encased ourselves in steel to get here.

We'll encase ourselves in steel to leave. How much of this world, these bodies, could we replace with steel or platinum? And what things are irreplaceable?

We descend into a basement, dirt-floored, something like a cellar in an ancient house. The machines housed inside the mill are stories high and sometimes miles long, and you can't take them in at once, so you constantly have the sensation of being a Lilliputian staring at the nose of Gulliver or the earlobe or the toe and not knowing how to put them together into something you can really comprehend.

We've been issued earplugs, and we need them. It's louder than a junior high school dance. It's the loudest place I've ever been. Even if you didn't have the earplugs, you couldn't hear the Director of Safety talking to you. We just walk from one thing to another in amazement, and sometimes fear, with no idea at times what we're looking at.

We walk around the corner of something that looks at first like a furnace. It turns out to be the bottom of the famous German caster. It spews out a tongue of brilliant orange light right there in front of us. The light is actually a two-inch-thick slab of metal at a temperature of more than 2,000 degrees. The slab is sliced off in a 150-foot length and continues moving in a progression of slabs to a tunnel furnace and then to a machine that rolls it into sheet metal, the kind used in automobiles.

The river of hot metal is gorgeous, riveting. You can look at hot metal that's 2,000 degrees; it's simply a charming popsicle orange. But you can't look when it's being melted in the furnace, where it's so hot that a glance would strike you blind.

There's just one human being at the foot of all this spewing fire—and he's writing numbers in a book. Where is his Paul Bunyan size? His bulging muscles and his health? He's nothing but a shade. He's thin and his skin is pasty, and he looks like it's been years since he's been outside in the sun. A shade has the form of a human being but is more like a projection, a hologram. He smiles at us and looks as though he wants to tell us about this baby he watches hours a day but it's screaming and stamping its foot so loud we couldn't possibly hear him.

The base of the caster goes hundreds of feet into the ground, and when you look up at the part you can see from this level, you see things that look like stalactites covered with blown-in insulation, like one of those foam houses of the future they'd have at fairs in the 1950s. They obviously aren't part of the design of the machine.

I take my earplugs out and yell at the Director of Safety, "What are those things made of?" He yells back something about hot metal drips and limestone.

Much later I'll realize they were stalactites formed from "breakouts," one of the thrills and dangers of steel casting. Hot metal, it turns out, has a skin like a thin balloon that keeps it from spewing out the sides. That skin is like the banks of the river, but it's just a skin. Unpredictably, the skin can pop and the 2,000-plus degree metal will burst in the caster and temporarily weld it shut. Sometimes it will burst through the machine and spill onto the floor or make these stalactites. What I'm seeing are the remains of hot lava that has run straight down eight floors. The "skulls," or chunks of congealed metal inside the machine can be removed with blowtorches and hammers. The ones on the outside they don't need to worry about. The machine still works.

This caster is a famous icon. It has a personality. It's studied by MBA students all over the world as a morality play. And here's the moral: Let the bureaucracy in your institution get too large, and the institution will get stale and afraid of risk. In traditional steel corporations, bureaucrats spent their time writing memos and reports as long as *War and Peace* explaining why this caster couldn't possibly work. Because proving it works by building it required risking an enormous mistake.

The Nucor Corporation was formed back in the post–World War II years when the world thought nuclear power was both dangerous and trendy. For a few years there were citizens from civil defense groups out all night scanning the night sky for incoming missiles, but there were also conferences held in Geneva to discover "peaceful uses of nuclear energy." There were people who thought our garbage trucks and iceboxes would be run by little nuclear boxes. The government kept nuclear generators cooling at the bottom of swimming pools and took them out for flashy occasions like the Geneva conference or the laying of a cornerstone on a building in Manhattan. Nucor was founded to make these things.

Of course, the dangers became clear soon enough, and the company had to find another way to make its money. In the early 1990s, Nucor had a visionary cowboy CEO who refused to be paid more than $100,000 a year, the lowest salary of all Fortune 500 CEOs. He had only three levels of management below him, and he knew the steelworkers and trusted them. His story is very American, very young, and very mythical. The risk is in fact what gives Preston's book—which tells the story of the start-up—its tension. Will this machine spew out a thin slab of steel as it's supposed to and then kick Big Steel and Japanese Steel's butt or will it keep on eating a million dollars a week in start-up capital? It's capitalism at its most thrilling. It's Rocky IV. This caster is the reason these students have come all the way from Japan, by way of Champaign-Urbana. It's one of the wonders of the MBA world. When they see the German company's logo on the caster, they nudge one another and smile and cheer. See? It was in our case study and there it is. It's real.

The Japanese students loved the German logo, but later, when we walk through the cold mill where the rolls of steel are flattened yet again and then coated with zinc, they'll see an enormous American flag hanging from the ceiling. I'll still be feeling particularly American and expect them to look at it with a kind of reverence. Instead, they poke one another in the ribs and point and chuckle. Why, when they're surrounded by all this power, do they chuckle? The radio is playing hard rock from a station in Indianapolis. The galvanized steel is falling in a steady stream from the ceiling; it's shimmering with silvery zinc and everything in the room is reflected in the watery surface of the steel. It's as beautiful as platinum, as polished silver, as the watches on the students' wrists. It's a waterfall of shimmering metal. What private joke are they sharing? They won't be able to answer my question.

I've felt so tough in here. Please understand: I had the world's most girl childhood. I liked to wear dresses. I loved my dolls. I learned to knit, crochet, and I spent days and months and years in fabric stores, staring into pattern books. The fabric store has been relegated to one aisle in an arts and crafts metaplex, but it's still entirely a woman's world. A steel mill is an alien universe to me, one that is entirely unabashedly self-consciously male. Preston's book is filled with German and American engineers, all men, drinking moonshine in bowling alleys and bars until dawn as they plan this thing. Women, when they appear in the book, are the wives of Nucor executives. Two other women appear in minor roles: one a grandmother who works alongside the men and is given a paragraph at the end of a chapter, and the other the first Director of Safety (not mine) who happens to be a woman, probably because they're hoping she'll be a good nurse and not authoritarian because there are safety violations everywhere by anyone's standard, and who has (as is always mentioned) beautiful red hair that falls out from her hard hat and who, at the moment of the most danger in the book yells, "Get off!" and not a soul moves.

So this is why I'm here, to listen in on the way men talk. The mill is one hour and one phone call away from the world I live my life in. I felt its foreignness as soon as I walked inside. Later, when we leave, one of the MBA students asks why she hadn't seen any women working there. "There are one or two," the Director of Safety tells us, "but you probably couldn't tell." There are women who work in the administration building who would never set foot inside the mill.

But maybe the otherness of this place isn't male. Maybe it's something else entirely. Maybe I just assumed it was male. Before I entered this building, I thought of steelworkers as men with bulging Village People biceps, a dirty rolled-up T-shirt, and a hand holding a hammer, all chest and arm. I didn't picture a face. You've seen those pictures of steelworkers in their beekeeper visors, wearing their silver fireproof coats, standing in front of the furnace with what looks like a sword. When the old busted-up wrecks of cars are melted down in the arc furnace to make this slab of steel, there are men whose job is to lance the steel, to inject the steel with oxygen—too hot at this point to look at, like the sun, without permanent eye damage— and the description is always like actually doing battle, like a swordsman fighting a fire-breathing dragon.

Even the caster is sexualized in reports of this mill. The thing that distinguishes this caster from others is the shape of the mold. It was offered first to U.S. Steel and Bethlehem, but they refused it, I'm told, saying it would never work. The mold is shaped like a vagina. They call it the vagina. It spews out hot steel.

The farther I got into the building, though, the less I sensed that machismo. It wasn't there. We were all human beings in the light of artificial suns, praying they would sustain us.

We're in front of an open warehouse door and the wind is blowing in and the air is thick with gritty ash. It covers our skin and clothes and it covers the paper I'm writing on and it covers the ballpoint of the pen so the ink skips, though it doesn't matter because the grit gets in my eyes and I can't see to write. In two seconds we feel dirty and sick. One of the students spends the next half an hour looking for something, anything, that she can use to cover her face. Eventually she finds a napkin by a coffeepot in a small room off another room filled with dust-covered computers. As with many factories that are still functioning here in the rust belt, you see more computers than people. I didn't see men with bulging biceps and large hammers. What I saw was machinery running itself and the occasional human being staring at a screen or a sheet of paper, like my house this evening as I'm writing this—everyone in front of a television or computer, all of us in some odd sense cyborgs: half human, half machine. The rolling mill the next building over, in fact, is a machine as large as a skyscraper on its side, and it runs on three levels of software.

Up another flight of stairs in the dark and dust, around a corner, we circle like Dante. We hear the arc furnace before we see it.

I've never heard anything this loud in my entire life; it thumps so that you can feel it as though it's inside your own chest. It's an awesome sight: a furnace that towers over you. It melts the chunks of iron, there are electrodes lowering into the iron, and it's hotter than the sun. There are fireworks exploding from the top of it, up one hundred feet or so into the air, and fireworks coming out the front and all the time the ka-thung ka-thung ka-thung and then the minor third of a siren going off and the Director of Safety runs across the landing and disappears through another door and we're all left there until another employee motions for us to follow around a corner and another man in a hard hat and spark jacket runs around a corner toward the furnace carrying a blowtorch like he's a firefly in the dark and there are metal drums where natural gas is burning in flames wherever you look and we're taken into a tiny room where there's nothing to see and we wait there through the sirens and the loud explosions and we can feel the sound of it in the floor, until eventually the Director of Safety comes back into the room as though he hadn't lost us, and we're happy to see him, and one of the Japanese students says, "You know, please excuse me for saying this, but we have steel mills in Japan and they're much different from this. Forgive me, but this doesn't seem to be a pleasant place to work."

The director laughs. He has a boyish smile. The controller I talked to earlier had a boyish smile. It's the smile I see on my teenage son and his friends when they've decided to pad their sweatpants with thick towels so they can sled off an icy cement wall into thin air with a ten-foot drop to the snow and I'm saying they'll break their necks and they smile at me with this same smile. It's a whimsical, kind yet condescending smile that says, You are such a girl.

"The compensation's good," the director says.

And it is. At this plant. And they get weekly bonuses. And because there are only four layers of management between any steelworker and the president of the company, and management is small and housed in a nondescript building, there's a feeling of camaraderie. This is what we do, this is how we're compensated, this is how we can do better. It's our company. It's dangerous work, but we're paid well, and there hasn't been a fatality in seven years. When there is one, it's horrifying. Hot metal melts the carbon in a human body before it even touches it. The inner light of the hottest steel, called blackbody light, can blister your skin just by reflecting off the ceiling or the walls.

"Anyone really afraid of heights?" the director asks. The woman I'm standing next to looks at me like, What next? "Where is he taking us?" she asks me, as though I have a clue. She's the one holding a napkin over her face. I shrug my shoulders. I try to look confident even though we're all secretly convinced that we've just escaped a potential nuclear meltdown or explosion of some kind, the whole building exploding and pouring oceans of liquid steel across the surrounding cornfields and into Sugar Creek, our poor pathetic bodies burned beyond recognition in a field-trip Armageddon, the Illini bus and my van, our escape routes, gone like a human hair held over a candle flame.

But we follow him. He's young, he's sweet, he has a master's degree in industrial safety, he wouldn't lead us into any harm.

The room we've been huddling together in while the building exploded was small and cramped and we're glad to leave it, though it felt oddly safe and womblike.

We've told him that there isn't a one of us who's afraid of heights.

Of course I'm afraid of heights. I'm terrified of heights. I belong back outside in the sunlight, inside my car, drinking a cup of coffee, and trying to imagine what goes on inside here.

Though of course I could never have imagined it. I had to see it. And at this point there's no way out but through.

Lord help me.

I am in a group of people crowded into a small space and being asked to move onto an industrial catwalk eight stories above a floor, level with giant hooks supporting pots full of hot metal. I am in a group of people being herded in a relatively dark space. What's at the end of this space? Where are we being taken?

I fall back on pedantry. I'm a teacher. These are students. Did you know that fascist architecture was inspired by modernist architectural aesthetics, I find myself actually saying to one of the students, aesthetics that were given voice by, among others, Le Corbusier, who was inspired by, among other things, the functional and massive design of technology: of grain elevators and airplanes and ships and factories. In order to mass-produce something, I say, you have to have a large and functional space in which to do it. This includes modern hospitals, which are designed on a mass-production model, and industrial farms. They have a certain powerful beauty, and this is a beautiful architectural space in some weird way, don't you think?

I find myself saying these insane things as I'm holding onto a steel railing for dear life, hoping that the wonderful and sweet and highly competent Director of Safety has inspected every inch, every single rivet of this catwalk and that that large hook will not run into it. I think about Preston letting a crane operator bungee-drop him from this same height and I tell myself I'm no kind of journalist.

Praise the Lord for solid flooring, which we finally get to. There are the usual drums of fire, but I'm used to that now, and lots of steam, and one hole in the floor a couple of feet across with tongues of fire shooting through it, though I'm sure it's supposed to be that way; it doesn't seem like random burning.

We're up at the top of the caster, Gulliver's head. We've been down at his toes and the furnace is, I suppose, his kitchen. The ladles of hot soup from the kitchen are being poured into his mouth, which is still above our heads, and there are two men pushing chemicals with brooms into slits in the flooring, adding salt to the soup, and again, there are flames here and there and we're glad when they motion for us to go down an enclosed stairway because the siren starts with its repetitive arpeggio minor third again because, as it turns out, it always go off when the hot metal begins its run across the ceiling to be poured into the caster and we can't be standing here when it does. This entire tour is well orchestrated so that we're in stairwells and internal rooms when anything really dangerous is going on. Watching us is like watching a group of toddlers in a parking lot. I get it.

The building for the hot mill is L-shaped, part of it the eight-story melt shop that houses Gulliver and then the part that houses the CSP machine, the robot skyscraper lying on its side. You still can't take it all in.

First there are furnaces shaped like long railroad cars, and in fact they're on rails. They fill with thin slabs of steel. They're the tunnel furnaces, and they fill with melted steel and then the furnaces move across the building. They move! Imagine the furnace in your basement stoking up with heat the first day of winter and then following you on wheels throughout the house. The steel is passed to these moving furnaces like the baton in the second leg of a relay race.

There's flame coming out the end of the furnaces, a flame that's yellow-green like the inside of a carpenter's level mixed with the orange of cigarette ash. The railroad cars fill and then move down toward the CSP, which rolls the steel into thin sheets and then wraps it into bales, like hay.

We run down a walkway by the furnaces. We're in a single line now, and suddenly it's incredibly hot. Our bodies break into sweat under the green jackets. It's a long walkway, about the distance of a football field. Think of how it feels to run along subway cars and look down at the tracks, and then imagine those cars filled with tons of sun—not sunlight, but sun plasma itself. Imagine how tightly you'd hold onto your child's hand or, metaphorically, your own.

And then we enter another room.

It's beautiful. This is where the steel in fact looks like a river. Because it's slightly cooler, you can see some gray in the orange, a very fluid stare-at-it-for-the-rest-of-your-life mix of colors, but still glowing liquid lava. You want to touch it so badly that you'd almost risk giving your hand to it. But the thing that's amazing is the way it rushes through the machine, from one end of the long room to the other, an orange satin ribbon of lava rolling in a giant take-your-breath-away wave of glowing platinum.

The CSP machine is a six-stand rolling mill, and each 150-foot-long slab of glowing steel is rolled into a 3,000-foot-long sheet. The MBA students are amazed by this and keep asking how that can happen without the center of the sheet getting thinner or the whole thing bursting out the sides. It's something to do with the magical property of steel itself, which can be rolled without changing width by even an eighth of an inch. Water pours from someplace onto the surface of the rolling steel and cools it as it makes its way through the building. The water turns to steam and some of it pours onto the floor. It all seems, as with the furnace, very un-controlled, Dionysian.

You see this thing, this amazing robot that pulls liq-uid fire like taffy, then cools it, and rolls it into coils of metal that are sent out to other factories and made into school buses and steel girders for buildings, and there are hardly any workers watching over it. There were men here in Preston's book. But that was for the start-up of this factory. Now the computers are watching over it. Now and then someone checks the computers, but there aren't even chairs in front of the screens. This is, as the controller had told me, "a computer controlled/co-ordinated event."

We leave the building and exit into a space sur-rounded by yellow fields. The sky outside is quite beau-tiful today, opaque and blue, not like the steel mill haze you associate with the earlier part of this century. This is good. This is fine. The sky is clear. In the end, I feel privileged to have seen the mill, to have walked through that process. Now I'm walking through another. It's late October and some farmer has cut the hay around the mill and rolled it into bales. Where are the farmers? I can't see them. They're sitting someplace right now, un-doubtedly, encased in steel. I don't see a farmer and I haven't seen a single steelworker, not really, no heroic human bodies engaged in labor. I've seen processes hid-den away and run almost entirely by machine, processes that these MBA students and I will run from as soon as possible, in the same way we've run from farms, from nursing homes, from hospitals, from death. We live inside of chrome and artificial light, in business suits, in cars and malls. We'll go home and take showers and brush and wash the ashes from our clothes.

SMOKE

FORD'S TOBACCO WAREHOUSE AUCTION, THE WEEK OF THANKSGIVING, 1998

The day the tobacco settlement was announced and the price of cigarettes went up sixty-five cents a pack, the burley tobacco auction in Madison, Indiana, went on as it had since 1916, which is to say, without a hitch. The farmers delivered their one hundred–pound bales of leaf, the tobacco company big shots drove up from Lexington in their expensive cars, and the warehouse bookkeeper drew up checks to pay the farmers for the year's crop. Aside from normal fluctuations in the quality, price, and the amount of leaf, the only real differences between this auction and last year's were the number of government officials who did not show up for the traditional opening day ceremonies and the fact that Paper Chase, Southwestern Tobacco's tagger, had lost his dog Buddy in a hunting accident the week before, and he couldn't stop grieving.

Paper Chase waited for the obligatory speeches. His shirtsleeve cuffs were rolled up to his elbows; he wore a vest. He looked like a clerk from the turn of the last century. His job is to check the bales for hot or nested spots and to tag them with Southwestern Tobacco's tags. He held a stack of the tags in his hands.

These speeches were something to be endured, but they're also important rituals to him; they tie this particular Monday in Thanksgiving Week to other Thanksgiving Mondays going back for years, stacking one Monday on top of another, like a marriage ties you to a family and to other marriages and to a certain community. Rituals are important when you've suffered a loss. For years, he said, Buddy had been his helper at this auction. He'd walk up and down the rows with me, he explained. I'd hand him the tag when a bale was sold, he'd jump up on the bale and place it right where it should go. Everyone here knew him. The farmers and the buyers both would bring him treats.

We all know each other. We even take on jobs together during the off-season. Last year me and the auctioneer and one of the buyers painted apartments. Buddy would bring us our brushes. There's nothing illegal about the tobacco business, but this is like a mafia, he said, a family.

I came down to southern Indiana to find the Easy Spirit shoe factory, but it had, it seemed, gone up in smoke after forty years. So I ended up at this tobacco warehouse on auction day in the middle of a different story.

So where were the well-wishers on this opening day of the burley auction? Where were the usual speeches? No one was there from Senator Lugar's office. No one was there from Governor O'Bannon's. Still, they called the traditional roll of politicians. "Will the representative from Governor O'Bannon's office please step up and be recognized?" Pause. "I see there's no representative from Governor O'Bannon's office." In 1998 tobacco became the one issue in American politics that almost everyone could agree upon. There was, it seemed, a clear evil in this country, and those responsible were gathered here in this tobacco warehouse in southern Indiana. No politician would want to be seen here.

Only the mayor of Madison responded. He had to be here. This is an industry that brings in approximately $21 million to one of the poorest areas in the state. After the money turns over five times, the mayor said, it's worth $105 million. Jefferson and nearby Clark, Harrison, and Switzerland counties rely economically on the tobacco industry. "This is a big day each year in Madison," the mayor said. "We hope that you'll continue to raise tobacco products and be a proud farmer here in Jefferson County. We hope to keep a commodity that is legal and profitable. This is one thing where families can work together—mom, dad, the kids.

"And now," he said, "let's turn this crop into money."

The light in the tobacco warehouse is purposefully dim so that it feels, when you enter it, as though you've just developed cataracts or as though it's twilight and you've forgotten to take off your sunglasses. "The light has to be even," Paper Chase explains. "I've seen days when the sun comes out, and they had to stop the sale for a while until it went back behind a cloud."

Although the system of baling rather than tying tobacco and placing it in baskets wasn't introduced in warehouses until the 1980s, and now there are bales of tobacco as far as you can see, it still feels as though you've driven not only three hours south of the state capital but several centuries back in time.

Clots of farmers, both men and women, dressed in work clothes, chat with the warehouse workers; they chat with the auctioneer; they chat with the seller's assistants. They've known one another as long as they've been in this business. You'd think they might be talking about the "historic settlement," but it doesn't seem to faze them. The settlement is clearly a tax that will be paid by the consumer. It won't alter prices at this level.

They talk about their families. They know one another's families and have for several generations. One farmer asks another about his father; he used to come to every auction. "He knows everybody and is interested in things, but he can't get around." They sip coffee and eat doughnuts provided by the warehouse association.

This is a festival, though a serious one. Their livelihoods depend on this day. Areas of the country where tobacco is traditionally grown are usually hilly, and the farms family-owned rather than corporate-owned. Tobacco is the primary cash crop, which means area farmers grow corn and wheat and beans, but most of the farms are too small, the areas of tillable land too scarce, machinery too expensive, the competition from corporate farms too great to earn any kind of living from grain. A seven-acre base of tobacco, on the other hand, can bring in a $20,000 profit, enough to get one family through the next year.

Many of these farms were, just a generation ago, nonprofit, self-sustaining family industries—growing enough food to raise the children who would go on and live here and raise the next generation and so on into the future. Tobacco was the only crop that brought in the money needed for doctor bills, for hardware, and for heating oil. So the opening of the tobacco auction was traditionally judgment day, the culmination of the summer's work and the recent harvest. Most of these farmers have been coming here their entire lives. It's as ethically complicated an issue as you could find. Older than the United States government, this economy has allowed small farms in southern Indiana, Kentucky, Missouri, and North Carolina to remain in families only by grow-ing an unhealthy, even dangerous, product.

The work itself has changed only slightly over the years. Tobacco leaf is fragile, as is most produce, and the production hasn't been mechanized. It has always been labor intensive. The biggest change is in the improve-ment of pesticides and insecticides. "When we was kids," one woman said, "we'd catch tobacco worms each morning. We'd pick them off and throw them down and stomp them. They were green and icky, and I threw them at my sister. One day they'd be an inch long and the next day they were as long as your finger. It wasn't fun, but if you didn't pick them off they'd eat the to-bacco in no time. We did this all summer long."

There have been other changes, but tobacco is still the primary cash crop for many area farmers. "We're gonna have to eat on last year's crop," another farmer says. "I don't wanna lose the farm. It was my dad's. My dad passed out and passed down. Passed out and passed on. I'm the only one left. One of my brothers works in a factory. My oldest brother got into horses."

The quality of this year's crop is good. The tobacco just blew up out of the ground and never stopped. It's clear the farmers think of it as a crop like any other, and a beautiful crop at that. They refer to it as leaf growing. "Look at other places—strip malls, factories, large farms owned by corporations. Isn't this a healthier way to live?"

one farmer says. "It would be a shame for this land to be anything other than what it is, and tobacco allows it to stay this way," he says.

WORX will broadcast the auction live. Right now they're playing "Killing Me Softly" over the warehouse speakers.

Do the farmers worry about the health effects of tobacco? Some of them smoke and some don't. Almost all of the tobacco company representatives do. If you ask a tobacco farmer, you'll hear this refrain: "Cancer causing? Sure, that's a worry. But if you live in the city, you've got that smog, and that's probably worse. Tobacco's just a scapegoat for a lot of things that are wrong. I think it's all exaggerated. They're expecting the tobacco companies to pay the world off, but they don't force you to smoke. I'm not sayin' smoke ain't bad for you. It probably is. If you do everything you're supposed to do, you couldn't do anything.

"They shouldn't advertise to kids, but if people smoke as adults, the way it's filtered now. . . . It's your choice, but you could smoke a pack a day and live to be one hundred. Ask my father. He smoked until the day he died."

"You know," a Kentucky farmer says, "I was married to a woman for twenty-two years and she left me and this nine-year-old boy. That bore on my mind, how she could leave our boy. So I sat on the couch for months and I smoked and smoked and smoked and I started having blackout spells. I was smokin' so many cigarettes that I wasn't gettin' any oxygen. I'm not condemning cigarettes though. It wasn't the cigarettes. I'm condemning me."

When the auction begins, it begins quickly, with the auctioneer, the buyers, the taggers, and the growers all moving at a near-run in the aisles between the bales. Everyone is surrounded by the tobacco itself—burley tobacco with its strong, clean scent as recognizable and pleasant as the scent of apples. As he walks along the bales, the auctioneer sings his chant in a minor third chord. The tobacco company buyers on the other side finger the leaf and bid.

The quality of the leaf is good this year, and burley is the second most popular tobacco leaf in the world. The buyers are from Southwestern, from R. J. Reynolds, from all the major companies. If all the buyers bid the same, the auctioneer gives the sale to one of them, each one in turn. Now and then they stop to open up a bale and check for rot. Farmers and warehouse employees and taggers follow along in line. Three bales a second, the crowd moves down the rows, listening. Paper Chase follows at the end, his hands filled with tags. He misses his dog like you'd miss a parent or a child. It's a busy day, but nearly everyone takes time to console him and to listen to his stories in the strangely filtered sepia-toned light of the warehouse.

The Growing Season

Floating

Your name is Tina. The factory you worked in last winter has shut down and moved its manufacturing division to Mexico. This spring you're floating. All winter long the earth has been locked up, fixed and frozen, and now it's starting to ooze and breathe and turn fertile, and you're part of that.

Early spring, it's good to be outside. This is hard, like any work, but fairly pleasant, much better than the factory where you were shut inside without windows. You stand in the barn and all day long you place the seeds in inch-square cubes of potting soil. You contain the ooze and muck of spring in geometric cubes inside geometric styrofoam rectangles: rows and rows and rows of one-inch squares. You take the flats of seeds into a greenhouse that's a full football field in length.

The seedlings float in water on a base of black plastic and the plastic is thick with green algae the color of antifreeze or fake golf course carpet. There's so much of it, it wrinkles like old skin or like the skin on top of boiled milk when you run your finger through it. The tobacco seedlings lift up from the muck, three-leaved like clover. The double-paned inside plastic of the quonset hut sucks in toward the seeds. It ripples like lungs. Everything is like something else here. Everything flows together.

Like rice, tobacco needs a good wet start. The farmer you work for has bought up base from several other farmers in the county; he's allowed to do that now, within a county, so he nurtures the seeds like this. Some of the farmers with a smaller base float the seeds directly in the ground and cover them with burlap.

You're the only local woman you know who does work like this. You work with a man named Jesus. He lives here for eight months, then returns to Mexico. There's another man named Eduardo. In the off-season, you'll go back to the factory, but you prefer this outside work when you can get it. Later in the season, others will join you. The farmer you work for is the largest tobacco farmer in southern Indiana. He floats the seeds for farmers all around him. You can take these seeds home and float them in your own bed.

All day long you plant the seeds. You're tired at the end of the day, but you don't mind. You can think your own thoughts. The weather's good. The land is beautiful and rolling, and just beyond that hill there's the river.

There are places where the water on the black plastic floor of the greenhouse reflects the plastic ceiling and, beyond that, the moving clouds so the semicircle of the greenhouse becomes for one moment a complete circle, with clouds moving both above and below you, the black circumference of space: every line that separates one thing from another disappears, and you feel like you're falling down into the sky. It's worth it to have that feeling now and then. You could fast and pray your entire life in some city and not experience it. When all it takes is one spring day, a flat of seeds planted in potting soil, a greenhouse altar, reflections of clouds fogging the surface of the plastic arch, the surface of the water, the algae, your own reflection, all of it floating.

Farm Wife

Some of us have old-fashioned tobacco barns. Some of us hang the tobacco in tiers, and we use cable. The cable came from the Purdue people. So you don't go up in the barn per se as people. You bring it in on big beams, and you pull the beams up on cable. Though a lot of farmers have workers who still climb up in the rafters and hang the stakes. It's dangerous work.

I don't speak a lot of Spanish, but we get along fine. Our little store has brought in food they like. They don't eat bread, just those flat things. Those hot peppers. When they first came, we wanted to have a big meal to show them we appreciated them. But they were very quiet and shy. We had given them what we like, but it wasn't right.

They're faithful people, good people, but I haven't pushed or asked them. I know a farmer took them to church, but I don't know how to do that. I thought about learning Spanish, but then I think why should I do that. We get along real fine.

I don't make them work in the off-season. I keep a roof over their heads and give them the pick-up. They don't

have any costs here, and every once in a while if I need
something, they'll do it for me. Usually I don't even have to
ask. I don't ever like to demean them or anything.

We have an old gentleman who has fruit trees, and he
said he's never had such good help. They're such small people.
We try to make sure they have coats and shoes. I'm not one
to ever throw things away, and sometimes I get out some of
my boys' coats from when they were kids. If they get sick, I
doctor them. If it's too bad for me to doctor, I take them to
the doctor, and he won't charge me.

I love this farm. My life blood is here. That tractor? It's
almost like it's part of us. If it breaks down, we're broke
down. It's not like a job in the city. If your computer
breaks, you order a new one. One tractor eats up years
worth of profit.

We have a husbandry feeling for the crops. I could care
less if there's a dandelion in my yard, but if there's an onion
in my wheat, I get mad. My brother-in-law lives across the
road, my father a mile from here. Could we make it with-
out the tobacco? We barely make it as it is.

Cutting

Burley tobacco is a beautiful crop; it towers over you,
envelopes you, it's not on a human scale. It's animal-
like, and the vein that runs down the center is thick and
pliable, like a real vein but woody, filled with gooey
brown nicotine stuff, pulpy and shiny. The gum is good,

it makes the weight, but it gets on your hands and in your clothes, and the day is hot and humid and you have to work eight to ten hours a day in order to bring it in. You cut stalks with an acha, a tool shaped like an axe, and you run the vein through a stake, six stalks per stake, and you ram the stake into the ground. For every stake you make twelve cents, about thirty stakes per hour, two minutes per stake. You put one stake in the ground and then you cut the next stalk. Now the tobacco is a golden green; in the barn it will be a red-orange pale pimento shade, a rich bronze. Later, when you house the stakes and then, when it's ready to bale, you strip each leaf from the stake and then sell the stalk at seventeen cents per pound. You bale the leaves and carry them to market. By the end of the process, you've touched each leaf and touched and touched it.

Housing

The stakes hang from the rafters and the leaves twist above your head, floral and tattered, a reddish gold. Tobacco leaves are cured in a barn after they're cut. It's all about moisture—too little and they dry out, too much and they rot inside the bale, turn yellow and sickly. Burley tobacco is cured by air drying. The tobacco in parts of Virginia and North Carolina is flue-cured, with charcoal. The flue-cured process was invented by a slave. His name was Stephen.

Two men work in the rafters, taking the pole and pushing the six stalks off with their heels. The farmers says they've been lucky for the past six years. No one's been seriously injured. The stakes are sharp and workers have lost fingers; one almost lost an eye.

The workers are young boys for the most part, young men. All are Hispanic. A teenager pulls his hair through a hole in his baseball cap. Another teenager wears a Harvard University sweatshirt from someone's cast-off clothes. It's a warm October, beautiful Indian summer, but several of them wear wool caps pulled down over their ears. Another worker wears a watch, a panama hat, a fuchsia T-shirt; his clothes are clean. You immediately assume he's the boss and when you want to talk to someone in English, he's the one you choose. But he only knows a few words. You realize how subtle the signs of class are—a watch, a hat—how much they determine how far you'll go in an immigrant culture, how many generations it will take to get from one place to the next, how many years you can save yourself by wearing a certain hat and learning a certain language. He speaks English. The Harvard sweatshirt won't do it, but the silver watch will. You're also brought up short to realize that you haven't taken these differences into account. Here are the farmers, here are the workers, you think, forgetting that while the majority of the workers are here from generations-long conditions of poverty in Mexico, that others are finding refuge from violence and politics in countries other than Mexico, that still others are looking for adventure, that some are fathers and some are only sons, that some have wives waiting for them at home, that there are differences in skill and intelligence, that some will move on to fields in Florida after the growing season and others will winter here. Here's the man in the fuchsia shirt, and here's Juan who works so hard it looks like he's fighting the tobacco, and here's Nino, from El Salvador, whose hands are ashy like someone fighting an infection, and he lifts his shirt to reveal a scar that is also ashy, his skin gray. He works hard, but he doesn't look well. He needs a doctor.

Where do you live? you ask. In a camp up in the hills, and they motion to the west.

Come visit, they say, we've got a stew cooking for lunch. And you say that the next time you're down this way, you will.

Stripping

The young men stand around a table in the middle of a tobacco barn. It's like a quilting bee, you think, but there are only men here. There's laughing, and some talk and sing. As the tobacco is taken down from the ceiling and the leaves are stripped from the individual stalks, the metal roof is slowly uncovered, letting in more strips of light. Skeins of red twine.

It's early November. The sky is blue, the river is silver, and the light in the stripping barn is an orange-warm firelight kind of light, the color of bronze holy light you see sometimes in Orthodox churches, reflected from the candles and the icons. And you're standing under thick leaves that hang above your head like skirts.

There's the sound of the baler, a hiss, like a steam iron. There's the sound of the generator for the baling machine and a soft murmur of Spanish.

One man rips bottom leaves from the stalk and he throws it to the man who rips the center leaves and then throws it to the right. The man who rips the leaves from the tip throws the stalks in a crib. Another man lifts the leaves and runs the air compressor that presses the leaves into bales.

Tobacco leaves litter the floor, something like deflated balloons. A single wet leaf is very soft, very light, like the underneath of an old woman's arm.

The leaves from the top of the stalk are second quality, the middle is first quality, and the bottom stalks are what is called the trash. Each kind of leaf will bring in a different price at auction.

For a minute or two the generator goes off and everyone gathers around it. One young man gets it going again by pulling on a string, like a lawn mower. He waves to the guy who was leaving in a mud-covered black truck to get help. It's a circular wave, like a lasso rather than a straight line. They laugh in English—hahahaha.

There's plastic tied to the rafters. When the wind blows under it, it expands like breathing. The wind breathes, a worker takes a bale and throws it down and the leaves breathe, all the breath around the table, the beautiful bronze light, the smell of tobacco leaves, the way you face one another around this common worktable, the stories you tell, the kinds of stories that create a culture in a certain place. This barn is a mile outside of the town of Bethlehem, where there is in fact an inn along the river. Why would you ever want to leave here? Why would you ever want to go back home?

The Camp

Black trash bag skirting underneath a trailer, the metal peeled up and back like wood shavings or the skin of an apple; the trailer is blue on top, a tin can underneath.

There's a bee on a Miller Lite bottle on the kitchen table, a plate of sauce, a table pushed up against the door to keep it closed; the lock is missing. The windows are broken or missing, holes in the walls are boarded up with two-by-fours.

The rabbit ears on an old television set are covered with aluminum foil, drawers are at an angle, the veneer is ripped off the kitchen cabinets. The wallpaper, a pastoral scene of geese, is halfway ripped from the walls, the blinds are askew. There's a large hole in the plywood kitchen floor, so you can see down underneath the trailer; there are open outlets on the wall, there's a hose coming in through the kitchen window for washing dishes; they wash their clothes out back on a stone. There are mattresses everywhere, one thrown at an angle, halfway leaning against a wall, in what is supposed to be a closet. There's trash on the ground outside—cans and wrappers. They've left lunch cooking on the gas burner while they worked; it's one thin inch of vegetable stew.

These are young men. They're away from their families. It's like a fraternity. They've come from poverty. Not all the camps are like this, but this one is. It's only a few miles from the interstate. You've probably passed this way. An employer might say it's expensive to provide even this, that the workers create the squalor, that they're paid far more than they would receive back home in Mexico, that conditions in the factories they've left behind are far more dangerous, and you can only do so much. A woman might say that in this camp it's because there are no women, because it's temporary, because there's no real connection to this place. A social worker might say it's because these men are voiceless, they're powerless, because they live in a rural area where they can't as easily blend in, because they're illegal, many of them, and don't have access to social services, that they don't speak the language, that we are all responsible for this.

Indiana Farmer

"Americans got big and fat and lazy. He wants money for beer and then he quits. But these boys," he says, pointing to a young Latino man standing next to him, "can cut 1,000 stalks a day. I get American boys, I have to bail them out of jail. A good tobacco cutter will cut 700 stalks. On this boy's first day, he cut 900. The Mexican boys come in, they work eight and a half hours, and they whistle when they leave the fields."

Is it legal? I ask him, and he says they pay the workers cash, that it's an expense you eat at the end of the season. You can't deduct it on your taxes, you can't report it, but the government knows. Much of the production that goes on in our economy is increasingly done by migrants, he explains. The vegetables you get at the market were picked by migrants; chances are the apartment you live in was built by migrants. It's the way things get done.

"In Mexico," he explains, "this boy would make $20 a week making speakers at a factory. He'd have to pay $20 for gas." But he saved his money and came here. It costs $1,000 to get someone to take you across the border, $400 more for the truck that gets you up to Indiana.

"We get a call from a lady in Winchester, Kentucky, when the migrants arrive each spring, and we drive over to pick them up. There's a woman there who finds the workers and distributes them to where they're needed."

It's a call that brings the farmers into a world that's antithetical to the ethos of the family farm, bringing with it guilt and pain and responsibility and complexity.

"The first time we hired migrants," the farmer says "it was hard. I didn't want to make the call, but I didn't have a choice. I had to get the crop in. But I was scared to death to be around them. I didn't think they liked me.

"But then this one here came up to me. My name's Phil, and they call me Philippo, and this one said, 'Philippo, do you have your mama?' And I said I didn't and he said me neither. And we talked about losin' our mamas, and then we went to Wal-Mart together, and I told him I'd fix up the trailer, and he could live out back and work for me. He's been here ever since. He's like my son."

"If you stop and think about it," he adds, "what is this country? It's German and Irish and African. We need the pot stirred up. We're stirring up the pot."

FORD'S TOBACCO WAREHOUSE, THE SAME WEEK, LATE AFTERNOON

More ethically complicated than the antismoking billboards or the tobacco companies make it seem, tobacco farming has allowed a certain close-knit traditional rural community to survive in the face of increasing industrialization, urbanization, and mobility. It's allowed communities to stay together, and for families to stay where they are, to nurture the place they are, and to preserve the land. Farmers claim that tobacco became a scapegoat that allowed us to ignore our other sins—environmental sins, sins of materialism and overdevelopment, our economic and moral sins, sins that are so buried we're not even at this moment aware of them. You can come up with your own list. And even though the farmers are a damaged third party in the tobacco controversy, they are outside the centers of cultural and political power and share, with the migrant workers they employ, a relative voicelessness. They can't afford lobbyists. They're from more sparsely populated parts of the country, economically disadvantaged parts of the country, and their voice is not a powerful one. We don't tend to think of the farmers as potentially displaced workers or think of alternatives for them. They're decent human beings, their way of life is healthy, but they produce and export an unhealthy product.

You could stop us from growing tobacco, the farmers explain, which would force in most cases a sale of our farms, but that's not going to stop people from smoking. Someone's going to grow it. You might as well have small farmers earning a living from it rather than large corporations or smugglers. And many of the substitute economies suggested to the farmers involve commodities that come with their own evils—hemp or riverboat gambling. One farmer at the auction said that Switzerland County, a large producer of tobacco, was about to get its own boat. Everyone else has a boat, he said. Looks like we're going to get one too.

Wendell Berry lives less than an hour away from Madison. His brother John was a state senator in Kentucky and former president of the Burley Tobacco

Growers Cooperative Association, as was their father, John Berry Sr. His essays, particularly those that have appeared in the *Progressive,* are probably the most thoughtful descriptions of the complicated issues involved in tobacco farming. "Why don't you dissociate yourself from this evil?" he asks himself in a mock self-interview and he answers: "Why don't I dissociate myself from automobiles? Because I don't see how to do it—not yet. And I don't want to dissociate myself from the world." He explains that the farmers "need a crop, or several crops, which can produce a comparable income from comparable acreages, which can be grown with family and neighborhood labor, and for which there is a dependable market."

Switching to fruits or vegetables or grain won't work for this region unless everyone in the region agrees to buy produce only from local farmers. Agriculture has become industrial. Almost 75 percent of the nation's vegetables are produced by 6 percent of the farms. Smaller farmers are competing with large farms as well as with, and this is true of factories, of course, produce grown in other countries where labor is significantly cheaper.

The agriculture department at the local high school is working on alternative commodities such as the growing of the fish tilapia in vats and ponds. Researchers at the University of Kentucky are working on alternatives as well. But in Arcadia the children of farmers have no interest in staying on the farm. Over and over, farmers and local officials explain that the kids would rather work at McDonalds than do farm labor, even though farm labor changes every day and fast-food work is repetitious and comes, of course, with its own evils. And when the children are old enough, if they're able, they'll leave for someplace else.

So in the end, this story, as is true of almost every midwestern story, is about the Fall from Eden, the discovery one more time that this is an imperfect, complicated world. Sinful actions can have redeeming consequences; the most well-meaning act can be destructive. This is also a story about that hidden hairline crack that exists in every human system, simply because all systems and cultures and relationships are created by imperfect human beings. Cultures tend to split apart as the result of pressures along that hidden crack, that fault line. The fault line itself may be the evil (as, in the case of the antebellum South—slavery) and the pressure good, or the pressure may be evil and the fault line simply that—an imperfection, a weakness, a tragic flaw.

There are increasing pressures along the fault line of the tobacco farmer's world. Some of the pressures are governmental. Some of the pressures are moral. Some are economic. Some of the pressures are internal and some are simply the pressures of the changing times: the siren call of a new century drawing children away from the region. Both farmers and workers find themselves caught within a system that, because of the illegality, calls for secrecy and transience, breeding a host of evils and problems for all the human beings involved. For a while still, the culture tries to hold on to a vanishing way of life with the least possible damage to the individuals involved. It isn't easy.

The tobacco settlement went through today but the auction went on just as scheduled. Paper Chase places Southwestern's tags on row after row of bales. He smiles and jokes with friends he's known for years. If you just stood right here, you would think of this as a beautiful world filled with light and fragrance and sociability. But inside, everyone knows, he can't stop grieving. Things will never be quite the same as they were before.

IN SOPHIA'S RED SHAWL

And I, my friend, used to be very sensual and sentimental. But my character has completely changed. I live now only in a metaphysical world, and I think of nothing except scholarship.

—*Schliemann in Indianapolis,* edited by Eli Lilly

My father sent me off to college with a pharmacy-sized jar of Darvotran.

It was the early seventies, and Darvotran was a combination of the narcotic painkiller Darvon and some who-knows-what tranquilizer. I also had a jar of the antibiotic Ilosone, to prescribe to myself whenever I felt like I was coming down with something, and an experimental blister pack of Quaaludes, given to me by my mother before they were known as a street drug.

I could have earned some cash selling those pills on the street. But I wasn't a pill taker at the time, and I promptly forgot about them. In fact, I didn't take one of the Darvotran until my senior year, when I had all my wisdom teeth extracted, and I took one of the Quaaludes to get to sleep one night when I'd had a fight with my boyfriend.

I also, right after the surgery, drank some airline-sized bottles of bourbon that I borrowed from my best friend. She had airline-sized bottles of bourbon because her family was seriously intellectual. The bourbon went along with the small press they ran out of the back of their house, and the discussions about dead presidents like Roosevelt and Truman at dinner, and the family's antique, room-sized oriental rugs.

My best friend's father was president of the Indiana Historical Society. He sent her clippings from *The New Yorker*. I was impressed and envious beyond belief. She would always, I was sure, be smarter than I would be. Even when, in one class or another, my grades were higher, I assumed there had been some mistake. There was the world of the mind and the world of business. Your background was from one or the other, and I was somewhat convinced at the time that your future was determined by genetics and the past. I couldn't imagine a connection between those worlds.

My father worked for a pharmaceutical company. He was an accountant, but we got our pills for free. I knew that I would never be an accountant, but I could get married like my mother. I was fatalistic. I was doomed to have a life different from the one I wanted.

But it was a year of the most amazing talk. My friend and I would take history classes and talk about history at all hours. We would take philosophy classes and talk about philosophy. We sat in a creative writing class, I remember, and argued about determinism in one another's journals. Remember, we were freshmen. Everything was new.

My friend's mother sent her some S&H Green Stamps, and since my last name was Schaefer and hers was Hawkins, we put the green stamps on our doors. We were a team. Even our professors expected to see us together. Hey Hawkins, where's Schaefer? You've got a paper due.

You have to remember these friendships from college, when the person you always were but hadn't recognized, or had hidden, is brought to the surface by someone else and finally you think you know who the face is you see each morning in the mirror. Your face, your true face.

My friend changed her name from Phyllis to Jean the moment she entered the university. She had always been a Jean, she said, but had lived her high school days as Phyllis. Her Phyllis days were over. She got contact lenses. Her deepest dream was to spend time talking about makeup and to have a social life.

I already had the contact lenses and the makeup and the social life and my deepest dream was to become an intellectual. I gave her popular music and she gave me poetry. I taught her about dating and she taught me about Kierkegaard. We were both deeply interested in both.

By our senior year we had learned what we needed to learn from each other and branched into other interests that would define us. But during our freshman year we never, for one minute, stopped talking. It is, I realize now, a kind of falling in love: an excavation of our selves that revealed both the past and the person we would become, an archaeology of the soul.

My father worked for the Eli Lilly company for his entire adult life. What does anyone know about his father's work? All I knew was that Lilly made pills, that when my father and his friends played poker in the basement they were all from Lilly, and that the red Lilly signature was on every bottle of medication in our house. I knew that Lilly insulin kept my mother's handsome brother alive until he had a heart attack in his forties.

I knew there was an Eli Lilly behind the Lilly but never thought about him and, if I did, I would have assumed he was a corporate fiction like Betty Crocker, a fiction who'd been aborted before he'd gained his virtual identity.

I grew up assuming that Lilly was, of course, the best pharmaceutical house in the world. Why wouldn't it be? I didn't know that there were any others. I had a vague sense that the salary my father brought home from this company was responsible for the new clothes I wore to school in the fall and all of my bicycles. I took for granted that everything in town had the Lilly name. I was a burgeoning intellectual snob within my secret self. I read Sartre's *No Exit* alone in my room as I took my regimen of antibiotics for strep throat and blamed my sense of disassociation on the medication and the strep and not on Sartre.

I argued with my accountant father about foreign policy as though I knew everything and he knew nothing. I really didn't have the slightest sense that just two decades earlier he'd flown innumerable missions in the tail end of a bomber flying over Mussolini's Italy. He was just a boy then. I know that now when I look at the pictures. I was, as a sheltered freshman, only two years younger than he had been when he flew those missions. For years now, I've been older.

There was really no such thing as history to me when I was a teenager. It made no real sense. The entire history of the world was something that loomed and breathed below the surface, but all I saw was the mirrorlike surface of the moment as it reflected my own shallow face. Eventually that surface would peel away or melt like ice and I would stand looking down into something infinitely rich and endless and fluid. But for a while I stood on a thin layer of reflective ice.

At the time I had no idea how quickly two decades can go in an adult life, how it must have seemed liked yesterday to him.

I'm sitting in the rare books room of a research library. In the center of the library there's a fountain and the stacks are built around a three-story-tall atrium, and you can hear the pounding water wherever you are and it's like you're sitting beside a waterfall. You can read about whatever fascinates you without distraction because you're all alone inside your head. The rush of water hushes you, sheltering your thoughts.

I'm sitting at an oak table and though there are two other kindred spirits right here with me, we don't speak to one another. One is looking through old letters and newspaper clippings and out-of-print books about the origins of a building at the theological seminary. The other is looking through the same kind of documents, but I can't determine what she's researching.

I've got a copy of the Leni-Lenape epic, *Walam Olum,* and a book called *Schliemann in Indianapolis,* and a book called *Prehistoric Antiquities of Indiana: A Description of the More Notable Earthworks, Mounds, Implements and Ceremonial Objects Left in Indiana by Our Predecessors Together With Some Information as to Their Origins and Antiquity.*

I open the Schliemann book and another book by a friend of mine who'd written about Schliemann. For some reason it's all so interesting that I make a strange sound in my throat, a gutteral *ahh,* and I realize I've made this weird sound so that everyone can hear it. I look up at the man sitting across the table from me and smile an apology. That's OK, he says, and he holds up a piece of onionskin from the file he's looking through. I did the same thing when I found this letter.

I look through *Walam Olum*. It's a gorgeous book on gorgeous paper and the original pictographs are drawn in ink, each one on a separate page with the Delaware dialect beneath it and then the English translation and then half a page of footnotes for each drawing. I read the footnotes.

So this is what I was heading toward when I was a freshman reading Kierkegaard and Sartre. Somehow they were always connected with something sensual, some boy with dark eyes who brings the book I've left in his room and drops it off at the desk in the lobby of my dorm. Susan, the oh-so-cool note would read, your book.

And now I'm reading footnotes and exchanging sounds of passion with a stranger in a rare books room over out-of-print books and anonymous letters. I'm pathetic. I realize that. But, truly, these are great footnotes. It's amazing to me that someone would devote a life to this. The pictograms for this epic were found on sticks in Indiana and they were given to a scholar at Transylvania University in Kentucky in the nineteenth century and the scholar supposedly heard the oral version from a man who told the story in the original dialect. Who dug up the sticks? A mysterious Dr. Ward of Indiana. No one's ever discovered who this Dr. Ward of Indiana was, though many have tried to. He's part of the undiscovered rush of history, underneath the visible surface.

There have been several translations of this epic, and there's the possibility that this whole story is a hoax, that Walam Olum is a fiction; in that sense the search for it is like the search for Troy or Noah's ark, the need to find the outward visible sign of the story's grace. The man who wrote the footnotes devoted years of his life to studying this one poem. He did archaeological digs. He searched for ideograms in Chinese that might be similar and then did research to discover whether the similarities were all part of this elaborate hoax or evidence that the tellers of the poem came across the Bering Strait from Asia. He sent scholars out to research the Delaware language and to determine the meaning of each drawing. In his footnotes, he'll discuss the slightest line, why it may mean the word "chief" and why it may not, what the alternative translation would be if it did not. It was important to him to know the truth.[1]

Walam Olum tells the story of the Leni-Lenape's migration, and it's the story of Genesis. There's the snake

---

1. Though this was a man who himself loved hoaxes. One time he carved a thin wooden object that looked like a one-dimensional angel with a bird's beaked head, and he attached two feather quill pens as wings and he gave it a name and wrote up catalog copy about the history of the piece and the awards it had won and he submitted it to a show of contemporary art at the Indianapolis Museum of Art to see if anyone would notice. He wasn't fond of modern art.

and the garden and the flood and a Noah named Nanabush who resembles Utnapishtim in the *Epic of Gilgamesh*. And then the begats and then the white men come and that's where the poem ends.

This epic is included in anthologies of Native American literature, with no mention of the scholarship that went into it, of the puzzle of its origins. And here's the original scholarship, on this gorgeous paper, with this gorgeous binding and ink that seems almost embossed, an artifact that represents years of someone's life.

At the top of an ocean wave coming into shore there's a bit of light and foam. It rides into shore in a rush and then crashes and is drawn back into the great green or aqua water. The moment you're alive is the light and foam. Why did this man spend all these years researching these two sticks? Why did it wake him up at night? Because there's a moment you realize that you're standing on that light and foam and you've been handed a gift. That everything you thought about the ocean is wrong. It was far more complex than you thought. When you were sailing on the lake at Wawasee as a child, all around you there were artifacts of former lives and you didn't see them. Now that you do, there's not much time. It's a short ride. You solve this problem or you pass it on to the next generation. Right now you yourself are the alive and conscious one, and this is your only chance to see as far as you can see before you're pulled back under.

Who wrote these footnotes? Who led the group of researchers and archaeologists and historians? The cover says the Indiana Historical Society. But I've spent the weekend reading a history of the Lillys. The footnotes and the introduction and the money and the energy all came from Mr. Eli.

He wrote four books while serving as president of the company, while manufacturing and producing the world's first insulin, the first supply of Salk's polio vaccine, supplies of penicillin during World War II, and then other antibiotics like erythromycin and vancosin, the last line of defense against resistant infections. The company developed a cure for pernicious anemia. They were, of course, the developers of Prozac. All because, I believe, Mr. Eli didn't see the world as split in two—the world of the mind here and the world of the body there.

In the late nineteenth century, pharmaceutical companies were still associated with snakeroot and elixirs. Drugs were handed out by hucksters at state fairs. It was only in the twentieth century that people like Lilly realized that scientific research could determine which roots or compounds worked against what, and how reliably, and made decisions to sell these things as medicines, and by prescription. Some medicines still have a plant base—certain anticancer drugs are distilled from the leaf of a periwinkle and antibiotics are naturally fermented—but some drugs are created in a laboratory.

So a company like Lilly functioned through the early twentieth century as universities are supposed to. Instead of scholar-teachers you had scholar-businessmen. Lilly's interest in archaeology was connected to the business of pharmaceuticals. In search of antibiotic molds, he hired researchers to send soil samples from all over the world to the lab on McCarty Street. In this way they discovered erythromicin, among other antibiotics. His studies gave him a sense of the richness of history, of the way that human beings form themselves out of whole cloth. When the Depression hit, he didn't let a single employee go. He found something for them to do until the crisis passed. At various points they made conscious decisions to keep their manufacturing right where it began. In fact, in 1934 Mr. Eli had a replica of one of the original manufacturing buildings built brick by brick by blowing up old photographs to room-sized proportions.

Where have all these amazing, quirky people gone? If they're out there now, please tell me. Or maybe it's the stories themselves that are amazing, and they've grown over time, as stories always do, becoming collective fabrications. Maybe Mr. Eli and his father are no more real, in the narratives we tell of them, than the nameless men and women who became the models for Aphrodite or Zeus.

But, still, there are the stories. Mr. Eli's father took a large dose of thimbleweed and almost killed himself when he was trying to determine what was wrong with a batch that had been returned. He also collected memorabilia of Stephen Foster. At one time he had to hire eight people full time to oversee the Fosteriana that he housed in a building behind his estate. People came from all over the world to see it, including Gertrude Stein and Alice B. Toklas. How weird is this? Gertrude Stein and Alice Toklas in Indianapolis looking at the original manuscripts of "Jeanie with the Light Brown Hair." And while Stein said Foster might have been a poet if he hadn't discovered melody, you wonder whether the trip was sincere or tongue in cheek, like a Pulitzer prize–winning poet on a vacation trip to Graceland.

When Mr. Eli's father died, he was the owner of two Shakespeare folios and a lock of Edgar Allan Poe's hair.

Come back. Come back. I'm here in this room in this specific library, not in the past. The table is shiny with varnish. The librarian leaves the room for one minute to show someone to the circulation desk and when she does, she locks us in. Nothing can leave here. These are first editions, original copies of letters, manuscripts. There are manuscripts in here by people whom I love. I don't mind being locked inside here with them if that will keep them safe, but I'm uncomfortable when I can't move back and forth easily between this world and the one outside of it.

I never met Mr. Eli, though I feel that I know him as well as I know my own father, who worked for him. I know him through what he did and what he chose to write about and what I can uncover from his past. I choose to write about him and he chose to write about Schliemann.

I pick up the second book. The same beautiful print, the careful footnotes.

Schliemann was a wealthy European who spent his life looking for the ruins of Troy. In 1869 he came to Indianapolis in order to get a quick divorce from his Russian wife. "No sooner had I left the shores of France than the thought struck me that in this great country and among this practical people a divorce cannot possibly require more than a couple of months, and in fact I found it so, because marriage is considered here merely a civil contract which must cease to exist so soon as it is violated by one of the contracting parties."

Indiana and Wisconsin had the more liberal divorce laws. Schliemann spent months away from archaeology, and while he was here he wrote letters and kept a journal that is in itself a kind of archaeology of this place and of Schliemann's mind. Lilly was fascinated by these accounts because he saw the connection between Schliemann's search for the historical Troy and his own search for the historical Leni-Lenape.

And for love. Lilly was divorced from his first wife and married happily to his second. His divorce isn't mentioned in the corporate history. Lilly was remarried. While Schliemann was here he unearthed his perfect wife by mail, writing to a friend in Greece and saying he wanted a Greek wife. His friend sent pictures of several women. "How like noble Paris I feel," fiction writer Michael Martone wrote years later from the point of view of his own mythical Schliemann in Indianapolis, "choosing among the goddesses." In this, he's seconding Lilly who wrote of Schliemann that "the romantic features in the stories of Homer had been running through his mind with extraordinary vividness during the Greek adventures, turning his thoughts to those of love."

The woman he finally chose was named Sophia. Her name was wisdom. Schliemann had twelve copies of her photo made. He fell in love with that photo and he handed copies to his friends. What did he want to know about Sophia before he met her? He wrote his friend:

How old is Sophia?

What color is Sophia's hair?

Where does the family live in Athens?

Does Sophia play the piano?

Does she speak any foreign languages?

Is she a good housekeeper?

Does she understand Homer and any other ancient authors? Or is she totally ignorant of our ancestors' language?

He waited until his divorce was final. He visited the capitol building in Indianapolis while he waited, where "the representatives behave much like school-boys, all chewing and continually spitting; many holding their legs continuously on their desks before them and all plotting the laws in the most summary and reckless way. Certainly I should not like to live in a country whose welfare is entrusted to such fellows. I saw them throwing paper-balls at each other and even at the speaker. . . . And there are no coffeehouses here." At one time, during the period he was here, the legislature seriously considered a measure to change the definition of pi, rounding it to 3.5 to make it easier to remember.

When he went back to Europe, according to Lilly, who accomplished his own great things with his second wife beside him, it was Sophia whose fingers helped him remove the ancient treasures, secretly and carefully, treasures whose richness "surpassed all belief; golden diadems, rings, bright gold necklaces, gleaming goblets, earrings and other objects" to a total of 8,000. There were silver tablets and vases together with curious pieces of copper and several vessels and bases of helmet crests of the same ruddy material, all of it "gathered together into Sophia's large red shawl."

The treasures of ancient Troy were discovered and gathered into wisdom's red shawl. Okay, I know there's something absurd about Schliemann and Sophia thinking they had discovered Helen of Troy's tomb. Schliemann dressed his sweet Sophia in Helen's jewels. They thought they had uncovered the royal tombs of Agamemnon and Clytemnestra and Aegisthus and made the three incarnate—gods entering the world in the flesh. And Sophia and Schliemann named their only son Agamemnon.

But still: Schliemann was single-minded. He loved knowledge intensely enough to give his life to it. He wrote well, in fact; the problem is that he lived out his fictions rather than writing them. He couldn't tell the difference. But he discovered, nonetheless, real treasures.

Lilly writes in his afterword that "the Trojan treasure remained in Berlin until the end of the Second World War when its hiding place was found by the Russians. No one has heard of it since."

The man who shows me around the factory knew my father. They worked together. In here? This building? Every day of my childhood my father drove here.

Everywhere I look there are men and women in suits, all someone's father or mother or sister. My father was one of them.

They could show me capsules or antibiotics or scientists in their labs, but they decide to show me insulin. Twenty-four hours a day the production goes on. Years ago there were boxcars filled with pancreases from the slaughterhouses in Chicago. Now the insulin is indistinguishable from human and is manufactured from the DNA of E. coli bacteria.

The technology that converts that bacteria into human insulin is as complex as the technology inside any computer in the world. Human DNA is inserted in the bacteria and then the strings, which look like chains of colored beads, are cut into a peptide chain and then restrung. There are centrifuges here and homogenizers to break open the cells, and then the insulin is purified in chromatography columns one story high.

Chromatography. You know the way water seeps through your handwriting on paper and breaks down into the colors of the spectrum? What was simply black is now all the colors of the rainbow. Or the way oil turns into colors in a pool of rainwater? That's chromatography, and that's the way the insulin is finally purified, by making its way through columns filled with resin.

This process is complex and automated. There are operators watching over programmable logic computers, watching the processes go on inside machines. This building I'm walking through is the major supplier of insulin for the United States. This insulin is shipped to almost every country in the world. The whole process takes place quietly, behind screens of glass with lime green astronaut suits hanging from hooks so operators can suit up if they need to go inside to correct a problem. The insulin is bottled in a separate building in a process that reminds you of dairies—aseptic areas with tubing and glass bottles moving on chains and men and women in white suits watching over them.

It was Mr. Eli who brought Henry Ford's techniques to the process of manufacturing pharmaceuticals. In addition to scholarship, he thought about this business, about efficiency, and the lives of the workers. He guaranteed them jobs; he made sure that retirees were visited every year of their lives after age seventy.

Before his second marriage, Mr. Eli lived unconsciously and after his second marriage, he lived with purpose. I've decided that this is important. You choose or you let it all slide by. It's the plans, and the working out of them. In walking through this insulin plant, I'm walking through the visible evidence of plans made long ago. That's the part of this life my father lived within.

Do you think about the fact that the work you do is saving people's lives? I ask a man in front of a computer, a man who will go home to children who have no idea how he spent his day. Maybe he has a daughter reading Sartre who wants to fly away from everything he stands for.

I always think about it, he says. One hundred hours of my life go into every one of those columns. All this insulin, he says. And all those diabetics who would die from the lack of it.

It's like the ancient stories. You may not need them now but someday there will be a moment when they'll save your life. So this is what my father did with his life. And when he handed me those jars of pills, he knew I would never take them indiscriminately. He wanted me to know that they were there if I needed them. If I were in pain, my hand reaching into that bottle would touch the hours and days he'd spent here. It was the physical evidence. He had no words for it.

In a week or two I should be done with this fabrication. Tomorrow I go back to exercising, I watch the trees bloom, I straighten my daughter's spring clothes and box up the winter sweaters. Someday, to someone, perhaps this stuff will be of interest. The spoons in my kitchen, the brass disks on the legs of my dining room chairs. And love? It was love that got me through from day to day. For language, for other human beings. Dig down deep into the dirt with your fingers. Discover something that might be healing. Some tincture of something that someone might need to live one more day.

I love the people sitting at this oak table because they love something enough to be locked inside with history.

I wrote in this essay about Eli Lilly and his fascination with Schliemann and about my friend Michael and his fascination with Lilly's fascination with Schliemann and now my own, all of us connected because we're writers committed to the history of this place. And there's more. You unearth history in order to find those depths in yourself and to prepare for the time when you're pulled back under by the tide. My friend Phyllis/Jean was the maid of honor at my wedding. A year ago she came back to Indianapolis, and I saw her again at her father's funeral. She was a wife and mother, and her husband was a businessman. We talked about our children, our families, and still, about ideas.

Over the weekend when I read Lilly's biography I discovered pages devoted to my best friend's father. There were pictures of him in the center of the book. It was Lilly who hired him to run the society. I remembered her house in Irvington, the books that were stacked on tables and under chairs, her beautiful sister and cousin and lively mother, and the way she loved her father and how sad she was when she noticed, one summer day, his aging hands.

Both my father and hers worked for the two different sides of the same man. In our friendship, in some odd way, we brought those sides together.

Or maybe it was more than that. What do we want most from our lives, if we're honest. I think it's someone who will come and live with us, however temporarily, inside the house we've spent our lives preparing. Someone who will be amazed at each room, each light-filled window, each thought wrapped in tissue and hidden in some closet to bring out as a gift to anyone who loves us well enough and can receive it. Someone who might excavate the memories when we're gone.

I love this library table and the sound of the fountain's rushing water. I love the life that exists outside of it. I love the books and the words inside of them and the voices who sang them into being. The universe is filled with mysteries and secrets.

SILO DREAMS

The miller crouched down between two metal pipes. A rabbit hole, the opening in a tree trunk. "What do they do in there?" I shouted above the pounding of machines. "Just mill around!" he said before he disappeared.

He looked like a miller from a fairy tale: dressed in white, a smudge of flour on his nose. What was I supposed to do? I followed him. Past men filling giant bags with flour. Past boxes of swine starter, riboflavin, and niacin. Past gray flour dust and wheat like ball bearings underneath my feet. Past black-and-white photographs of the mill with a model-T and horse-drawn wagon out in front of it. Past a wooden locker painted with a red star and crescent moon. Past a curve of wall that echoed the curve of the railroad track outside, past waving plastic strips like the entrance to a carwash.

Suddenly, everywhere I looked, there was vertical motion: an elevator that was nothing more than a wooden floor with open pulleys, buckets that rose up and down on honeycomb stairs, and man-lifts the width of a step that you can jump on with one foot and rise ten floors fast—like you've ingested yeast.

Then through a door, and I was looking at seven flights of stairs that lead to the top of the silos. The silos. Outside, a blinding silver-white, but inside, dark and dusty and metallic. All seven flights of stairs were covered with seeds. There were holes in the floor where they released cyanide gas earlier in the century to kill the bugs. The cyanide spread in clouds into the city.

Back then, the miller said, you'd see people working here with only four fingers. They had no good way of keeping the gas from escaping. The equipment wasn't safe. But it was anything for industry.

And then suddenly we were in sunlight. From the roof you could see the river and the Speedway and all of downtown, even the top of the new milling facility in Beech Grove. Last week, he said, I was in the restaurant at the Hyatt. I could look over here and see what was going on. I could see Junior loading up the truck.

The wind picked up a swirl of grain dust, and it blew in our eyes. The miller laughed and waved away the dust. You see? he says. That's why they want to get rid of us.

Earlier, we'd walked through a sunlit room that housed the flour sifters: twenty or so wardrobes arranged in two straight lines. They were suspended from the ceiling and up from the floor on black rubber stems.

Every one of the wardrobes shimmied, continuously, at 160 revolutions per minute, twisting around on the rubber *stems with a motion like belly dancers. A part of the con-crete block wall and all the glass windows shook with the sifters. The oak, the sunlight, all of it was vibrating, all of it golden and yellow as pollen.*

Inside the wardrobes the grain fell through metal nets with a thread count as dense and fine as percale sheets. The bran swirled like sparks when the miller opened the ma-chine and pointed his penlight. Outside, stainless steel trucks lined up to take the flour to other cities. Over 34,000 bushels of grain were processed here each day, most of it from local farms.

A year ago, I walked with the miller through the silos and now the silos have been blown to smithereens, and nothing I could say or do made one whit's differ-ence. It's as though the silos were never there.

You live long enough in one place and you watch it change around you. If I were to move to this city now, I would think the place had always been the way it is, that it's eternal and I'm the one who changes. You stay in one place, though, and you see the ghosts.

The silos that used to be here were built in 1918, one year before Gropius opened the Bauhaus in Weimar, Germany. Seventy years later, the silos would end up at the center of a controversy that would involve the entire community. During the controversy Bauhaus aesthetics would be invoked, argued, and at times misunderstood. For a year the poor silos would become a symbol, and they would teeter between two centuries. The city would want to tear the silos down and build a theater. They're building a theater, an Omnimax, and the park that surrounds it will look like Venice. There's been an industrial clear-cut. Good riddance.

But I'm such a nostalgic. If something is the way it is, I tend to want to see it stay that way. It is, I acknowledge, a flaw in my character. I tend to think that if you hold on to something long enough, like an old car, eventually there will come a day when it gleams with mystery. I tend to see human artifacts as expressive and to think that once the artifact is lost so is the expression. There's no longer a word for something. Without the image, in this case, the mill, left around to set a certain strand of feeling resonating in the human heart, that strand of cultural wisdom is lost.

The new plan for the area centered around images that had no inherent connection with Indiana's *past,* but rather to its place in the *future,* a future that would privilege fiber optics and virtual experiences, and electronic connections between the park and the citizens of Indiana. In describing the Omnimax in 1993, one comissioner was rhapsodic: "It fills your peripheral vision, your seat leans back. There's high resolution, the film's right there, you can retrofit it with 3D, you can add on as technology changes."

"The world is a fast moving train," she added. "If you don't leave the platform, it'll leave without you."

In the early nineties, the city was interested in predictions about the next century, as though predictions could control it. They passed out packets of newspaper and magazine articles featuring futurist Faith Popcorn. She was the park's Nostradamus, and the future, according to Popcorn, was in the microchip, in the wire. In other words, what was literally in this space was not as important as what was virtually within the space. They could build Knotts Berry Farm (at one time a plan for the space) or Euro Disney as long as it looked anything but industrial or agricultural, both old world, old century, and as long as it had phone lines. The city was clearly on the side of progress and the future. If there was any other side to this argument, they were sure it was founded on greed or well-meant sentimentality and was, in either case, misguided.

Opinions among people ranged from "the silos are magical, monumental" to "they're an eyesore, a bunch of concrete slabs. Get real." There were arguments about whether these particular silos were historically or aesthetically significant.

Industrial architecture is, I'll admit, an acquired taste. And I've acquired it. When the mill was built, it was a state-of-the-art facility for the entire country. Architecturally, it was still a good example of a daylight mill—large amounts of wall space devoted to windows, the corners rounded to keep clean of flour dust.

It was also one of only two flour milling facilities left in the state. But the argument was never really about the significance of one particular site. It was always an argument about a symbol.

What made the clash interesting, and in many ways moving, was the way the silos brought out both optimism and fear of change, two feelings that always need a symbol at the end of a century. What lies ahead is either a "rough beast" that should be greeted with fear or something new and marvelous waiting to be born.

A grain elevator is a powerfully ambiguous symbol, like a centrifuge that sucks in meaning. It's a symbol of rural as well as industrial America, both in its combination of materials—concrete and wheat—and in its function: one elevator can store the annual produce from a hundred farms.

Like all late-nineteenth-century American industrial architecture, elevators were built to be, simply, functional. No gingerbread, no curlicues, no symbols, and as such they were the poster child for European modernism. At a time when Europe wanted to blow the past away, here was a vernacular architecture that unambiguously and unself-consciously did that. It was all function, and form followed along meekly, simply, and, to European eyes—beautifully. How do you build something beautiful? The American answer seemed to be that you try to be like God, to build something that works, where the flesh fits around the soul like shrink-wrap.

When photographer Eric Mendelsohn first saw American grain elevators he wrote his wife that they were "mountainous, incredibly space conscious but creating space. . . . I took photographs like mad, Everything else so far now seemed to have been shaped interim to my silo dreams. Everything else was merely a beginning."

The father of the International style, French architect Le Corbusier saw the grain elevator as the "first fruit of the New Age." And so the American elevator went to the Bauhaus and came back to us echoed, years later, in the pure geometric forms of the architecture all around us: in the state office building, the top of the Hyatt, the mirrored cylinders of Keystone at the Crossing. The International style is displayed, as writer Tom Wolfe says, "50 to 100 stories high in the cities and in endless vistas in the shopping malls of the new American suburbs."

Grain elevators represented the brave new world of science and technology, the hard, clean abstractions of science, free of bourgeois ornamentation. Le Corbusier thought that the universe *outside of the organic world* was hardwired for order, that it was the architect's duty to align himself with that rational mathematical beauty, to scrape the organic messiness of the world away, all that mortal moss and gunk that obscures the purity of the inorganic universe. "For all around us," Le Corbusier wrote in his manifesto *Toward a New Architecture,* "the forest is in disorder with its creepers, its briars and the tree trunks which impede [the architect] and paralyse his efforts."

Grain elevators satisfied that need for order. Their form and their spacing across the American plains were as rationally determined as the rest of the midwestern grid. Grain elevators and railroads are responsible for the way the Midwest looks even now; towns were spaced along railroad lines at determined intervals, and elevators were the valves determining the flow of grain, like blood, from the heart of the country to its extremities.

And still, of course, they were built to hold grain— messy, unpredictable grain for our messy, unpredictable bodies. Grain that sprouts and harbors bugs and heats up and explodes. Grain that behaves, in bulk, like a solid and then, mysteriously, like water. "I have seen," Reyner Banham writes in his book *A Concrete Atlantis,* "a twelve-foot cliff of red durum wheat in the hold of a ship in the Buffalo River, standing at what was clearly steeper than its natural angle of repose, suddenly let go and flow like a wave around the legs of the men working in the hold."

If you were looking for a symbol that would contain both the natural world and the industrial, both longing for the retreating wilderness and the optimistic vision of early industrialization, you couldn't find a better one. It was that resonance that was at the center of this controversy, a controversy over symbols finally, and a strange, ambiguous, ethically convoluted symbol at that.

Reading *Toward a New Architecture* now is a strange and at times terrifying experience. Le Corbusier's vision was a utopian one that, with the world wars, turned sour. Early modernist architecture was in itself about order and erasure. It was, finally, about control on a massive scale. It was about high-rise apartments and technology.

Italian writer Edoardo Persico wrote rhapsodically about the opening of the Lingotto Fiat factory in 1927. It doesn't read the same way now as it would have then:

> At morning, dominated by the stare of these great glass eyes that have the impassivity of justice, the workers wait under the hollow cyclopean walls. They do not speak, they do not move as they would in other human assembles; they wait. All things are in order, nothing can be changed, everything obeys an order which is not the expression of human will but of a wisdom submissive to the Laws. They await the Laws. . . . They have more need of order than of bread.

The dark side of modernism was of course fascism; whether it was inherent in the aesthetic or was a style easily co-opted by dictators, it was an architecture whose purpose could be used to subdue, to assert power. They were intended to be about a kind of order that would lead to human happiness, but these buildings were in fact both beautiful and impersonal and they became, after the 1940s, symbols of darkness. They turned into the impersonal looming presences of a Batman movie. It was painfully clear to everyone that Hitler's final solution was an industrial solution.

The postmodern had to win, no matter how hard you try to associate silos with bucolic innocence. This isn't one farmer's storage bin; it's a corporation's storage bin. You could retain it only with a wink, a nod, as an ironic quotation.

Indianapolis is now a thoroughly postmodern city, which means several things: that the cultural construction of all identity is assumed, that our deepest wish is the creation of a perpetual motion machine disconnected from any source of power but its own, an eternity created entirely in culture—a world where Disneyland exists, as critic Baudrillard noted, in order to give everything around it the illusion of the real. We are "people formed by language and climate and popular songs and breakfast foods and the jokes we tell and the car we drive," as Don Delillo wrote in the 1996 novel *Underworld*.

The facades of the old buildings were retained when they built the new downtown mall in Indianapolis, but it was just the facades. The fronts of buildings were propped up on toothpicks for months and then they were stuck like postage stamps onto the corporate surface of the core.

The new city is a play of surfaces and symbols referring only to one another, not to a recognizable indigenous past, and somehow during this fight over symbols,
the silos were destroyed on schedule and replaced by the
Omnimax. The mill I walked through a year ago is
gone, and so is the old city. The new one is bustling and
exciting, I'll grant you that. It's pretty and clean and almost utopian.

Human freedom is limitless, once you realize that
any ordered world is all a brave construction, a fragile
building that can be *re*constructed as you wish, that
identity can be consciously constructed as a mask.
Though it's in the slippage between the created mask,
the illusion, and the real identity (assuming of course
that there is a real identity, a human community that has
integrity and beauty and history) where evil enters in.

But that's another issue. My problem, now, is that I
want to know where my miller has gone. I'm a nostalgic,
and while I'm fine with the fact that there will be a line
of school buses in the parking lot at the Omnimax, that
there will be schoolchildren living in some virtual
Alaska or virtual nineteenth century within its theater, I
miss the sound of the machines in the mill, the feel of
real grain under my feet, the taste of real bread.

I walk by the place where his mill was, and there's a
shower of sparks pouring around the side of the one
brick wall that's still left standing. There's a giant machine that looks like some kind of metal bird, picking

up bits of metal and wood with its beak and placing them in a giant dumpster. The tip of the bird's beak presses the refuse down and then turns on its revolving base to find more trash. It's a cold, wintery day, and I don't see a single human being. There's just the cold and the crane and the metallic postapocalyptic trash.

I was going to take a walk along the canal, but I can't do it. I head back to my car. It's just too weird to hover between two centuries. I'll be glad when the mill is all gone finally, and it's spring. I'll be glad when I've forgotten about the miller, when the memory of him is just the ghost of one of the many layers of history hovering above this ground, as insubstantial as the swan boats that will soon float on the canal, carrying mayors and commissioners and people with their cameras, down along the river. One hundred years from now, for some nostalgic writer, they'll be what always was. Someone, somewhere, will mourn their passing.

S(T)IMULATION

If it has a flavor, we have the extract of it.

You wish you had an extract of his scent to pull out on a day like this. So gray you need all the lights on in the house. It's been raining a cold rain for hours, and every twig of every deciduous tree and every pine needle holds a heavy pearl-like drop of silvery moisture at the tip, like a bead of varnish or hardened glue. The sound of the rain isn't above your head, on the roof of the house, say, or in the trees. It's more of a gurgling beneath-the-surface sound, like the sound of water through buried pipes and sewers.

It's enough to drive you mad. You draw the house around your shoulders like a shawl. What was the smell? Was there, in fact a metallic coppery note, like pennies? Decaying grass, a hint of musk? Maybe lemon zest and marjoram.

You wish you could remember. You had a shirt that for one whole day was drenched with the scent. It didn't last, but maybe you could reconstruct it. It wasn't artificial, not any kind of manufactured thing. It was in his skin. But you think you could reconstruct a simulation. The materials are someplace in the house; if you could only find them.

You take out the pots and bowls, the rack of spices. You suck on anise seeds or clove. Your grandmother used to feel like this. She told you. Is it absurd that you still feel it generations later? You know it is. But you're sick of this subtle landscape, of playing it safe. The gray skies, the three straight walls of this interior midwestern state with only that one loopy line of river to the south. The equally straight-walled counties and the rational grids of streets and rows of corn and unimaginative gravestones. You open the bottle of powdered sage, but there's no fragrance. It tastes like household dust. How did this happen? It's been on the shelf too long. You wish for a great passion that would split your world in two and then re-form it. What's wrong with you? You have free will, of course. You could take off in a plane. Instead, you wish for the days of traveling salesmen carrying canisters of ground cinnamon. You wish for anything but this late spring blandness.

You need adventure. Put the pots and pans away and get in your car. Drive beyond the fishing lure factory, where they make the parts for artificial worms. Head toward Floyds Knobs, which almost look like mountains.

Go past the Cement Farm where you can buy white plaster animals of any genre for your garden. Around Santa Claus, Indiana, stop and swim in the giant bathtub with the wave machine that simulates the ocean. Accept that it's not quite real but revel in it. Then get back in your car and drive to Brownsburg.

He's standing there surrounded by the burlap bags of seasoning. Do you see him? How did he stay so young? Your grandmother described him just like this.

Here's the story of pepper, he says as though he expected you. It's almost as interesting as vanilla.

Does he really believe that? Did he ever?

The outer room of his factory is lined with seasoning. The scent is strong. There are other women here, you notice, buying tins of herbs. He looks just like his father, one woman says. And his grandfather, says another. And his great-grandfather, says a third. The great-grandfather was in a rock band before he started selling spices door-to-door, she says. He saw a need. Women needed them.

Needed a rock band? you ask.

The spices, of course, she says.

A rock band in 1902?

Whatever they were called then, the woman says, and she turns back to the great-grandson.

Who is twenty-five years old and deeply handsome. His great-grandfather sold sweet vanilla to cloistered housewives.

Our vanilla is the best, he says, nothing artificial. The beans are dried and crushed and soaked and then distilled. In France they soak the dried beans, he says, in sugar. We soak ours in alcohol. American vanilla, he says, is over 30 proof.

So sell me some, you say, please do, and make it real.

Each vanilla bean is lovingly tattooed, he says, by farmers. He holds a dried sweet bean and you inhale. You smell your grandmother's kitchen, the French toast you made for your son when he was in preschool, back before your entire family became so tired of cooking food.

They're woven together in pieces like a blanket, the beans. My grandfather, he says, followed spices into every major country in the world. He presses buttons on a map. Press peppermint, a light comes on in northern Indiana. Sage, a light comes on in Yugoslavia. Cloves light up the world in Zanzibar and Madagascar, and pepper comes from India. Nutmeg lights up some islands with an unreadable name. This is, he says, an old map. Some of these countries, he says, might not exist. Like Indiana, you say to him, and he smiles as though you may be right. It's completely fabricated to make airplane rides from one coast to the other seem interminable.

Years ago, he says, this building was the Thompson Sled Company. They made the red flyers. Slick blades of metal that glide through snow. Now everything in the building, every sheet of paper, smells like pepper mixed with cumin.

The great-grandson tells you that he works part-time as a model and producer. He finds beautiful girls in shopping malls and enters them into contests—Miss USA, Mrs. USA, Miss Universe. Spice-making is no longer a full-time job. The contests are owned, he says, by Donald Trump. That's why Miss Universe will be held the next three years in Gary. Can you imagine it? he asks. Donald Trump and Gary. It's because he owns that riverboat there. He wants to change it from the murder capital into a different kind of sin.

You like that he said sin. According to the map, Gary is surrounded by oceans of peppermint. You can almost taste it.

We have a girl performing in Korea now, he says. His brother models full time in Los Angeles and New York.

It's a beautiful family, a woman says to you.

He lived for a while in California, the woman says. He had a job lined up at Euro Disney but couldn't learn French in the three weeks' time he needed to. So he's here again, surrounded by bags of cilantro and turmeric, tarragon and thyme, by pasta sauce seasoning and jerky marinade, by Netta Belle's formula for dry rub barbeque.

He seems to float above it. Do you have a crush here? Crushed and dried and ground and flaked. His great-grandfather showing up at your great-grandmother's door when things are at their most bland and change-less, offering her a choice of spice. No wonder she seemed to like to cook. No wonder she presented those cakes so lovingly. I'll take all you have, she said, and more. I have this batter mixing in the kitchen. What does it need? A bit of this and that, she'd say. I'm sure you have it in that bag you carry.

The great-grandson has filled the lobby of the spice factory with things that make him laugh. Antique type-writers, a bowling ball without holes in it. Why? Have you ever seen a bowling ball without holes? he asks. It was a mistake someone made. He likes mistakes.

There are photographs of his great-grandfather with Colonel Sanders. They were best friends, the great-grandson says. They met when the Colonel drove up to the spice factory. He was out looking for a place to put a chicken restaurant. They developed the chicken season-ing together. In the early years, the factory's chicken sea-soning was called Claudia Sanders Chicken Seasoning.

He's filled a birdbath with gold coins—*cinqo cin-talles.* You've never seen such wealth. It overflows. You need ninety-eight of them to make a penny, he says. Everyone who comes through here takes one. I filled it with the money because I got tired of filling it with water. It's not, in some ways, he says, real money. Pepper, he says, was one of the oldest forms of money. Battery

Park in New York was originally leased with the rent to be paid in peppercorns.

He says: We like to give gifts out with our spices. His great-grandfather gave coffee urns to every women's group that sold thirty-six dozen bottles of vanilla. He gave out filmstrip and slide projectors, New Testament record albums—twenty-six records in simulated Bible leathers—the "finest American flags," and Nesco Electric Roasters, Samsonite folding metal tables, addresserettes and checkerettes. Church basements all over the Midwest are filled with this stuff, long after the spices have been consumed, the old women who dusted the spices on their chickens and made the cakes for church banquets long gone, the freshest spices in the world unable to preserve them.

In the 1950s he gave out multispeed tape recorders with the sale of fifteen dozen bottles.

Think of the thrill you and your fellow members will get from recapturing those precious moments of music, sermons, important meetings, and discussions. The thrill.

The great-grandfather carried out a one-person war on artificiality.

The best cinnamon in the world came from Saigon. He recognized the coming crisis in 1964, and he stockpiled bark. We're burning a lot of trees, he said. The jungle would smell, in places, like burning cinnamon.

He wrote an entire book on vanilla to prove to the world that vanillin, or artificial vanilla, was not in fact a true vanilla. "No more so," he wrote, "than if a dentist were to make a set of artificial or false teeth and holding them up to the world declare . . . This is an imitation man!"

So where do you make the vanilla now? Where do you grind and bottle the spices? you ask the great-grandson. He takes you back into the factory, and there are ancient silent bottling machines and a silent pepper-sorting machine. (Sneezeless pepper, he says. It's the dust and twigs that make you sneeze, not the pepper.) And there are two men lethargically scooping herbs from one bag into another.

We make the vanilla in the back, he says. We never take anyone back there, he says.

Don't let him fool you, one of the men says. We're growing marijuana underneath that pepper sorter.

Can I just peek for a second into the vanilla room? you ask.

No one can see it, he says.

So describe it to me, you say.

Stainless steel vats, he says, and tubing. Like a brewery. So you don't want us seeing, you say, that what you're running is a still.

There are no clinking bottles of vanilla, and the workers seem like characters in a historical reenactment. You get the sense that when you leave, they'll go back to playing cards until the next woman talks her way back here.

The men laugh and continue scooping thyme.

Dear Mr. Summers: May I express to you my thanks for the expeditious handling of my recent order. . . . The clocks are just exactly what I wanted—an excellent example of American craftmanship.

Sincerely, M. C. Westmoreland; General, U.S. Army

It made my great-grandfather crazy, he says, when they stopped making silver coins. He truly couldn't bear it. He said the money was debased and fast becoming the only money in circulation. A peppercorn is something real, and so is silver, but these sandwich coins were something else entirely. They still minted a few pure silver coins in 1965, the great-grandson said, but Congress passed a law saying that those last few would carry the date 1964. Which meant, he said, that from that year on there wasn't a single thing you could count on.

So his great-grandfather made these clocks and called them The Numismatics to celebrate the passing of the silver era. Twelve silver coins to mark the hours were embedded on the dial.

Uniquely designed to show all three of our last silver coins, it is the only clock that truly says "quarter past the hour . . . half past one . . . a quarter to . . . "

In 1964, or thereabouts, the cinnamon burned, the coins were simulated, and the world changed into something new.

I'm bored, your son says. It's the rain, the interminable weekend. He's spent the last two days sitting in front of the computer. He's got a new game called Sims where he creates a virtual shadow self. He's play-acting his adult life. He and his shadow are both named Dave. Virtual Dave began with nothing and by the afternoon he had an apartment with two televisions and one sink.

Real Dave is a teenager, and somewhat secretive, so it's with some joy that you realize he'd give you access into virtual Dave's life. He lets you watch him go through his entire day. When Virtual Dave needs to wash his hands, you notice, he has to walk into the kitchen and those extra steps almost make him late for his carpool.

You need a sink in your bathroom, you tell him, the real mother interfering in the virtual son's life, and he says he can't afford one and still have two televisions, which he wants, he says, more than sinks. Of course, you say. I understand. They're only virtual germs, he says, and you get real points for watching television in this particular world.

In the afternoon real Dave comes downstairs to tell you he's been promoted at work. Correction. It wasn't "he," it was "I." "I've been promoted," he says. He can now afford the extra sink, and he thinks his flesh-and-blood mother will be happy. Virtual Dave has neighbors and potential girlfriends, but he doesn't have a mother. One morning you had one son, and now you have two, and this computer son doesn't seem quite ready to live by himself. For instance, he doesn't pick up his pizza boxes or his underwear. You have to remind the real Dave to manipulate the virtual one to do things like that because he's losing quality-of-life points. Don't you know how this game is played? you ask him. You feel that at some level you've failed him. You wish you could disappear into *Star Trek* glitter and insert your cartoon shadow self into the screen and teach him a few things you still haven't taught him.

Flesh-and-blood Dave's real sister watches her virtual brother go through his daily routine. She comments on his choice of clothes, the time of day he takes a bath, the kind of car he drives.

At about 4 in the afternoon, his sister comes to tell you that the virtual Dave had met a girl and he was scheduled to propose within the hour. You both go upstairs to watch the proposal.

She's a brunette. Where's she from? you ask. He doesn't know. The game doesn't tell him that. But he met her at work.

She seems like a nice girl, you say.

For the rest of the day, you notice that the real Dave walks into the real kitchen to wash his hands. We have two sinks! you say to him.

At night your real son comes down from the computer, depressed. I just burned down my house, he says. How? you ask. A fire, he says, from the new propane grill. Do you have insurance? you ask, and he says he hadn't bought enough.

I'm sorry, you say, and he says he'll just begin the game again tomorrow.

You could transfer every act, every thought at every point in your life somehow onto the computer. You could live forever like this, burning your house down and not caring. Years could go by when you live like that, pushing your virtual self from here to there. And too the memory of the scent. How many days of your life have you wasted, living in some dream world? What system do you use to find what's real?

Sims get the most gain from "high-quality" objects. That is, a small TV is less efficient at entertaining than a large TV. . . . Part of knowing your Sims well is in directing them toward obtaining and using these high-quality objects. Get 'em working and get 'em shopping!

The Sims world is one of interactions with objects, whether those objects are other Sims, plants, or lava lamps.

Your son walks by and sees you reading his manual. You're reading the manual to my game? he says, and he starts laughing.

And you're taking notes! he says, and he looks over your shoulder. You are! You're taking notes!

You feel of course foolish, but it's not the first time.

You? Enough of this charade. *I.* I feel foolish. I'm the one living today in some memory. It's midsummer. It's sunny today, not raining. This is nonfiction, not fiction. My real son's name is Steve, not Dave. And I'm the one trying to reconstruct this imaginary scent when I'm surrounded by all these real ones.

Did you read it? I ask him, hoping to go on the offensive and he laughs and says no, and I tell him I can answer any questions he may have about the game.

I haven't read it, he says, but I don't need to. I have this thriving Sim.

Some day you might need to go back to the text, I say, and he just rolls his eyes.

I thought your house burned down, I say, and he says he'd been exaggerating. Just the porch burned down.

So, I say, are you married? And he says he's thriving in his professional life, not his personal one.

So she turned you down, I say, and he says his Sim isn't that good at relationships.

What does he do? I ask and he says he's in internal affairs in the army. Soon he's going to be promoted to general.

Congratulations, I say, but what I'm thinking is why the army when you had all those other choices. The government lets you sign up for the army when you're only eighteen years old and nothing your mother says can stop you.

I go downstairs and get a bottle of real vanilla extract from the cupboard. I take it back upstairs and tell him to inhale. Snap out of it! I say to both of us. There have been some hard spring rains and now the grass needs mowing. There are weeds in the garden. Let's get outside this house and work this precious weekend. Or run or take a walk or play basketball, it doesn't matter. Let's just get outside the house, I say, and breathe the air. Tarragon and nutmeg. Basil and oregano.

Quitter! If you're really not happy with the Neighborhood, just click on the Quit button to depart the Sims world of dynamic fascination and return to your own. Look around you—are you making the right choice?

There's an ozone warning today, he says. The real air, he says, smells like automobile exhaust and burning rubber. I like the air-conditioning, he says. I have my computer in here, he says, and my TV and the telephone. He points me to the manual. *The Fun motive is fulfilled when a character is entertained by something: TV, stereo, pinball machine, pool table. The Energy motive is fulfilled by sleeping and by drinking coffee.* Go take a nap, he says. I tell him that I'm tired of sleeping. *If you unchecked Free Will and don't direct your Sims to sustaining activity, they can suffer Needs failures, and can even die!* Right now, I say, we're going to do something fun. Let's bake some brownies, I say. I have this bottle of vanilla. Until I do something with it, it will have this bitter taste. If I leave my computer now, he says, my Sim will die. Do you want that on your conscience? I'll take that chance, I say. *The household autonomously mourns over the urn (or tombstone, which the urn becomes if it's taken outside) that now carries the earthly remains of your Sim. After twenty-four hours, you can direct the mourning yourself. You can move the urn to a place of honor, or dishonor, if you like. If you're truly napping on the job, and let everyone in your household die, the house will be available for sale in the neighborhood.*

CARBOYS

Even his own son acknowledges he married too young, that he wasn't ready for the responsibilities of marriage and children. He fell in love with engines as a boy, and as in that fairy tale where a piece of ice lodges in the young man's heart and changes him forever—the sound of engines, the feel and heft and smell of them, was his ultimate concern. As though that first sight of an engine entered through his eyes and became a small but powerful version of itself grafted to his soul. This inner version was more perfect than anything that he could see, and it wanted to replicate or release itself through his hands. The engine. The sound of it drowned out human voices. He could never escape it. He had no choice. It was the power that drove him through his life.

He was raised on hoop-barrel farms, which means his father moved the family every year, chasing virgin stands of straight-grained elm. Elm splits easily and can be shaped into barrels, which were the things that—before boxes and plastics and cheap mass-produced glass—you used to haul and to store every single fabricated product. A hoop maker made barrel hoops wherever the elm grew. He'd use up an entire stand of elm and then move on.

The boy grew up with that kind of restlessness. When he tried to live his life in one place, he would leave and then return home. So his life had that particular shape, the one like wheel spokes.

He made his first engine when he was eleven, a tiny steam engine using 8- or 10-gauge brass shotgun shells, with slightly altered pennies as the pistons. The engine was an oscillating cylinder type, soldered onto a tube that was soldered to a one gallon-kerosene can. The kerosene can was the boiler, and it blew up frequently.

He sold engines to his friends and when the engines proceeded to explode, he insisted that no one was ever seriously hurt, though, he wrote later, "A couple of mothers were singed while their son's engines were running on the cookstove and the boiler ruptured."

They were of course just mothers, slightly singed, just one of those necessities you bring along on the heroic childhood journey: food, water, fresh air, hair of newt, one mother.

Once he was molding molten lead on the stove while his mother was canning fruit. The wooden mold was wet from the weather. When he poured the lead into the mold, the moisture turned to steam and split the wood. The hot metal landed on his mother's hands. She was in the middle of canning. It was hard work. It was summer. It was hot. There was boiling water and glass and hot sugary fruit. She'd just moved the entire family by wagon with her precious dishes packed in the wooden barrels her husband had made. She had four children. And in the middle of this, the hot lead on her skin, the interruption in the chemistry of canning—the precise temperatures and timing.

Later in his life he will remember the spanking he received as a result of the explosion, but won't mention that his mother was in pain. In fact, when he writes his memoirs, he doesn't mention her at all once the metal is spilled on her. It's spilled, that's it. Hot metal in a kitchen, and he goes on in the next sentence to talk of engines. That's his remembrance, which is of course a child's remembrance and one his mother might have wanted him to carry. Forget her scream. He was a favorite son. She loved him more, perhaps, than she loved her husband. She let him melt metal while she canned her family's winter supply of fruit. She let steam engines hiss away on the stove top. She named him Clessie Lyle after her favorite doll, a doll she'd named. The Cummins he inherited from his father.

There were all these boys like this, born in or coming of age with the new century. For a young, white male in the United States, the early twentieth century was a prosperous time, a good time to be young. When these young men reached their twenties, the whole country roared. Their girlfriends cut off their Victorian hair.

So much new technology to choose from then, so much power and so much freedom. For hundreds of years nothing had happened in science and technology, and then all of the sudden there was the gene and the double helix and quantum physics. It happened all at once, and anything was possible. Human beings woke up from some amazing sleep and spent the century trying to decide if in fact the dream was better.

The technology of choice for boys was the engine. Nothing domestic about it—you wouldn't use it to power your mother's iron, like electricity, or to wash some clothes or cook or to have some interminable he said–she said conversation, like the telephone. No, you put the engines on wheels or hulls or runners and you hung outside the house in what used to be the barn and the sound of them was greater than a chorus of human voices and when you got the engines right you let them thrust you with as much speed as you could manage— anywhere, anywhere—to an important meeting with another boy to solve some pesky piston problem or around in circles to see how fast you'd go or across the country to prove that you could do it.

The Midwest at the beginning of the twentieth century was like Silicon Valley in the 1980s. There was a critical mass of inventors working on similar problems. Each one found, through trial and error, a niche. Or they competed until one drove out the other. The key thing was that they were young, they were obsessed with new technology, they had confidence, and they knew one another. A problem raised by one was solved by another. There are pictures of them in one another's family albums—visiting at the lake or in each other's workshops. Ford and Edison on their trips out West, Cummins and Ford lifting a diesel car up to the second floor of Ford's workshop to test it out, Teetor and Duesenberg and Cummins and Studebaker hanging out with their wives at Lake Wawasee in northern Indiana. In many of the pictures, the men have their hands on one another's shoulders.

Most of these guys didn't go to wars. Their lives were different in that century than those of other men. They stayed behind and made the machines the boys in troops required. When the wars were over, the technology had been fine tuned, the factories had grown.

They were a kind of brat pack and at the same time there was a brat pack of midwestern writers who also knew one another and who watched and listened. Booth Tarkington wrote *The Magnificent Ambersons* to chronicle, as chroniclers do, the effects of the engine on his midwestern city. As far as I can tell, the inventors who were contemporaneous to Tarkington were so lost in the spinning joy of engines that they never seemed to think about effects. You can do it, so you do. No brakes. We'll have no brakes on here.

In those days, cars were made by hand, one at a time. They were made without bodies for their road tests, and the test drivers sat on temporary seats out in the rain and snow and they drove around the city, even up and down river levees.

Some companies have histories connected to a place, myths and stories. I love the stories of Clessie and his financier, the richest man in southern Indiana.

Where to start?

When Clessie first saw W. G. Irwin's Packard, it was up on blocks (to save the tires) and covered with linen tarp. Imagine treating a car like that. Even the tires were wrapped in paper. Like a chocolate individually wrapped in special foil, the car wasn't something to have two or three of, to be leased and end up at some wrecking yard. It wasn't, in other words, off the rack, not yet; this was a Packard—designer made with shining engine blocks and paint that gleamed and all of it wrapped and stored, like a wedding dress, in linen.

Clessie had never driven a Packard, though he told Irwin that he had. He weighed 110 pounds, and when he tried to turn the crank to start the car, he couldn't budge it.

Then he remembered that small, two-cycle boat engines could be rocked against compression and started without cranking. He dipped a cloth in the gasoline tank and opened the priming cups on top of each cylinder. He squeezed a few drops of gasoline from the cloth into each cup and turned the engine crank back and forth enough to suck the gasoline into the cylinder. He closed the cup valves and rocked the engine two or three more times with the crank, hopped onto the driver's seat, wiggled the spark advance and retard lever back and forth, and the engine started.

The Irwins only needed a part-time chauffeur. In the winter, the job disappeared and the Packard rested on its blocks. It was a summer toy. The Irwins got him a job as a motorman on the interurban line they owned. Simple enough, an interurban. You go from one place to another on light rails and electricity, a nice domestic trolley. But in places the interurban rail ran parallel to the Pennsylvania Railroad, and of course there were boys running them and of course there grew up a rivalry between them, and of course they tried to race one another and of course the steam train always won when they hit the sparsely populated area between Columbus and Seymour and both cars could go full-out.

So Clessie found a way to get more speed by bypassing a voltage controller and doubling the number of volts from the trolley kite on the straightaway. Between

Columbus and Seymour, Indiana, with passengers leaning out the windows, the interurban raced the train and won.

Using Irwin's car, Clessie rigged a belt from a cider mill to a wheel and turned on the car. While his friend poured the apples in the mill, Clessie sat in the seat and advanced the engine, which worked until he hit fourth gear. That's when the mill exploded and cider and apple pulp went flying through the garage and the car's interior. The beloved car.

And after that he came up with the idea of removing the rubber tires from the Irwins' touring car and replacing them with wooden and then steel rims with flanges, like a railway car's. He invented a device to lock the steering wheel and drove on the railway, with W. G. and all the terrified Irwin management, from Columbus to Indianapolis and back. The car went up to sixty miles per hour on the rails, sailing through Jackson and Bartholomew counties like a bird. The faster it went, the more solidly it clung to the rails. Can you imagine the excitement? An off-rail vehicle—a 1907 open Packard touring car—that could be converted to a private railroad car skimming on the rails.

Of course, in the end it wasn't safe. You needed the brake system and steering for the road, but the brakes had a tendency to lock when on the rails. You had to stop periodically to hook a telephone up to the railway telephone box to make sure you weren't heading for a train. It wasn't practical. But that one exhilarating test was worth the risk. The bankers went along for the ride but gripped the seats. Are you sure about this? Slow down. Slow down! The thrill.

And did I mention he'd recently been married? 1910? The night of Halley's comet? That he moved, with his wife, to Indianapolis for a more steady adult regular job again at Marmon? A steady. Adult. For the rest of his life. Everyday clocking in. Regular job. In 1910.

In 1911 his first child was stillborn. He was married like a grown-up. His wife was depressed about the child and he didn't quite know what to say to her. He had married too young. She expected a certain kind of life. He was confused and anxious. He had a job and had to be there every morning. He was a boy still—couldn't people see that? It was too much, too much.

He was married, in fact, to the idea of engines. That was his first marriage. He'd try, he'd try, but any love outside of that one felt adulterous. Engines hummed inside of him, they woke him up in the middle of the night in a cold sweat. It was an idea inside of him and if he didn't act on it it would make him crazy; if he didn't act on it he would carry it throughout his life, which would speed by like a railroad car, so fast, and it would turn to something so heavy and dark it would blot him out; it would die inside the shell of him, stillborn like the child, and he himself would die outside of it and God would always remain angry with him for letting the idea die with him.

Noah, do this now. Don't ask why. So he built an eighteen-and-a-half-foot boat powered by a gasoline engine and floated it on White River in Indianapolis, the largest landlocked city in the world. He felt the need for a change of scenery to clear his muddled mind. He had grown up following elm trees from one place to another, packing up and moving someplace new.

Why not travel down the Ohio and the Mississippi to New Orleans in my new boat? he asked himself. Why not? That kind of life was more real to him than this smothering domestic one.

He was a boy. When I say *boy,* I mean the archetype, not something you're condemned to by biology particularly; I mean Jung's eternal one, that boy. The boy who likes to spin in circles, fists up in the air. The one who flies above the ground afraid of commitment to a person, to a place. If I don't really marry you, if I don't really make this house into a home, he thinks, then in fact I'm always starting over and if I'm always at the beginning of something, then perhaps God won't notice that the years are passing and I'll never grow old and above all I will never ever die. I'm eternally fifteen years old, you see? Something in the universe takes care of adolescents. I will always have my life ahead of me. There's time enough for decisions. I'm mischievous. How can you help but forgive me. I have, as you can see, this charming smile. You see this boat I made? I don't need to caulk the seams above a certain point. Today it's sunny in Jeffersonville, Indiana, and the Ohio River is slow and sluggish and I built this boat with my own hands and look, she floats. Of course she floats. How could it be otherwise for me.

But he and his brother-in-law didn't take a map. It was the beginning of winter, and I'm sure they told themselves they would outrun the weather. After all, they were heading south.

But they had never been in a boat on the Ohio River. They had no idea how to navigate the locks and canals near Louisville, one hour away. In the first hour out they were almost killed twice by passing steamers; then they hit a barge and lost half of their provisions for the trip. They went down a dead-end canal, and the locks were impossible.

But they kept going. Clessie's diary is filled with the kindness of strangers and roasted ducks and befuddled coon hunters and cold and terror and bailing water and caulking holes with Brainard's cast-off shirts. Brainard, like the mother, is there to swell the scene, to supply the shirt, to highlight Clessie's nature, the natural foil.

They made it to New Orleans. It was a foolhardy trip. They rested for two days in Louisiana and then took a steamer to Tampa, Florida, where they would—with the luck of boys—find their first jobs there: parts as movie extras in a melodrama. Sultans and damsels and Moorish architecture and costumes and sunshine and the aqua-blue waters of the Gulf of Mexico when 1,200 miles away where your wife is waiting the sky is gray and brooding.

But eventually they have to come back home, and by the time they do, Clessie has invented a new stuffing box for marine engines that he wants to market but he gets his name in the paper again by building a motorized bobsled for frozen rivers and testing it on the city streets.

Other than that, he tries to settle down. The prodigal surrogate son, he opens an engine repair and machine shop in W. G. Irwin's garage in Columbus. And then World War I begins, and he gets government contracts in part through Irwin's contacts. He machines tools for a company that makes hand and rifle grenades; he makes hubs for artillery wheels. He outgrows the garage and moves to an abandoned factory and keeps working throughout the war.

Diesel fuel is a grade two kerosene refined from crude oil, one step up from the kind of kerosene that's used in jets. It has a higher flash point than gasoline, a more predictable flash point, and so it's less volatile than gasoline—you'll be pleased to know that the next time you're in a plane. Boats that blow up on the water usually are the ones with gasoline engines.

And diesel produces less carbon monoxide than gasoline. Don't try this at home, but you could lock yourself in the garage with a diesel engine running for a day or two before it would kill you.

The characteristics of the fuel demand a different type of engine. A spark plug begins the combustion process in a gasoline engine. In a diesel, there's an injection system that turns the fuel to vapor, and the heat is created by compression. The injection system and the timing are the keys. It also creates more heat per gallon than gasoline, which means that it can work in heavier engines, which can in turn haul heavier things. So it's a perfect fuel for farm machinery and ships and, eventually, trucks.

After the war, there was an interest in diesel engines because the Germans had used them successfully in submarines. Clessie talked the Irwins into buying a license to make a diesel engine based on an original German design, but with a unique injection system, Clessie's system, which he designed and patented. Diesel engines existed before Clessie Cummins, but they weren't good for much of anything. It was Clessie who perfected them.

The patent was one part of his genius.

The second part was showmanship.

One December he began a 10,000-mile nonstop, nonrefueling marathon on the Indianapolis Motor Speedway track. Again, it was the beginning of winter. The weather was horrendous. He and his fellow drivers would take turns sleeping on the floor of the truck. Sometimes they would fall asleep at the wheel. The grandstands were empty and ghostlike. This was the Roman Coliseum of race driving, the monument to speed and danger and adolescent thrills. Around and around the circle in a truck: again, the rush, the rest of the world disappears, and you're just left with yourself and the engine until the boys began to "see apparitions at night in the fog . . . the ghostly visions of men who had crashed the wall or smashed over it kept looming out of the mist."

"For two days and nights," he writes, "the pea-soup fog persisted. Flare pots borrowed from building contractors . . . their dim yellow glow barely provided enough of a guide to steer by. . . . One driver became hypnotized and nearly wiped us out. Headed straight for the concrete abutment supporting one edge of the bridge over the track near the north turn." But they kept going. At one time they discovered the torque was too loose on the engine caps, and they rigged a screwdriver up to a long pole and one of them hung out the edge of the car while the others held onto his feet, like a scene from some action movie, the car still turning around the racetrack and the one who'd drawn the lot tightening the caps upside down in the freezing wind.

At times they got goofy, little boys drunk with the monotony and the freezing mist. You might be one of the adult official witnesses, fresh from your warm bed and your real world sanity, called out to spend your requisite hours sitting in the stands and watching to make sure Clessie didn't for one second stop and you'd be pelted with banana peels thrown by the giddy boys in the passing car. Clearly, you'd think, they'd lost their minds.

But the engine in the truck came through: 14,600 miles without a stop.

"When you grew up in Columbus, and you needed a job," one worker told me, "you knew you'd have a place at Cummins or at Arvin or at Cosco.

"Cummins was a small town company, and people loved it. When you started there, you felt that it was MY company, with a capital 'M.'

"People assumed they were at Cummins for life, that they would be loyal to the company and it would be good to them in return."

Sometime in the early 1990s, capital—always fluid, always finding ways, like a virus, to replicate itself—began to move. In a global economy, without the commitment or even the sense of a particular place, its history and its meaning, capital will pull out or, in order to keep the company from going under, will move to where it's cheaper to build the objects.

I talked with someone who's been to Cummins factories in third world countries. Cummins is a good company; they make a good product. But when it comes to third world countries, they're like a lot, if not most, American companies.

"The companies in Brazil," he said, "though they don't have OSHA looking over their shoulders, they're a lot like American factories. You can't tell much difference."

"But in Juarez," he said. "I felt sorry for those guys. Seventy-five cents an hour is what they make and they sit there all day in the acid fumes you use to clean metal before you solder. All day long, heavy soldering with these smoky fumes that you can see rising up around their heads. Over several years, it's enough to kill you."

In 1919 when Cummins began, the engines were made by hand. Even by the 1930s, the company would make fewer than one hundred engines a year. A modern engine factory will make over one hundred a day.

What Cummins has going for it now is the design of its injection system and a sense of its history, an attempt, a *hope* that it can remain woven into the fabric of a town. Even now, each one of the engines is made according to specifications of a specific customer—subtle differences in torque and engine performance. And there's still a loyal workforce. The average seniority of the workers is more than twenty-seven years. But there are fewer employees than there were ten years ago, and the sons and daughters of these workers have had to look elsewhere for work. The man who shows me around the plant is retired with four children. All four of them have left the state for professional or service jobs someplace else. The men and women who worked here in the fifties and sixties assumed their children would "get on at Cummins." But it was in some ways a Camelot, and it lasted for only one generation.

The plant is, largely due to union efforts, a much cleaner, well-lighted place than factories in, say, the forties. The walls are white, the lighting is good, the floors are clean. The workers wear safety glasses and earplugs and there are no fumes, not even, really, a recognizable odor. It's a pleasant place to work.

Much of the work on the assembly of the older engine, the N14, is still done by hand but with of course power tools, and there are belts that move the engines. The engines look like black coal cars; they move along the line from one worker to another. There are lines of black electrical wire hanging from the ceiling, attached to the tools in assembly workers' hands. Workers tighten main bearing caps and steady the cam shafts as they're inserted in the engines. The iron engine blocks come in from Mexico, but some of the machining is done at Cummins by hand. They work at an even, pleasant pace. They smile at one another and joke. You can tell they've known one another for a long time.

For some reason, I'm struck today by the look of people's hair. The styles, the precision cuts and color, the care with which all this hair has been arranged each morning, the thought of each assembly line worker going to Great Clips on the weekend and each morning, using a blow dryer and gel and looking in the mirror and having enough money to buy the products that are made in the factory two blocks down the road. They spend the weekend at the mall in Edinburgh, taking their grandchildren to soccer games. In the novels of the thirties and forties, these same men and women would be working in impossibly dangerous conditions, conditions that would be in sharp contrast to the pastoral goodness of the farms they left behind.

The sons and daughters of the assembly workers in those forties novels are these workers. They have benefits now: health insurance and vacation. There's even a company country club. Everyone who works at Cummins has a membership. There are company picnics and pop machines and an arc of cheerful blue neon light welcoming them to the break room. Outside the factory, there are buildings designed by architects from all over the world, the architectural fees all paid for by the Irwin-Millers. Even the fire stations are beautiful.

When they retire at a decent age, if their health holds, they'll have a decent life. Golf games in the afternoon, breakfast with their pals at Bob Evans in the morning, trips to Gatlinburg and Florida, maybe even a cottage in Michigan.

There are roadways with white lines crisscrossing the 1.3 million square feet of the Cummins Engine Company

factory and a constant scurrying of fork lifts—ten or
more moving lifts wherever you look, ferrying engines
from one place to another—from the lines where they're
assembled to the place where they're painted to the
enormous washing machine where the water throbs
against the glass windows exactly as it would in a laun-
dromat. So many fork lifts, little cars with their own
hidden engines. In one place there are even stop lights.

But still, it's a human place. You'll see a table with six
incredibly beautiful metal pistons sitting next to Diet
Coke cans next to pictures of someone's children. The
"big shots" work in glass offices that you can see from the
factory floor, and it doesn't even seem like working. They
stare at computer screens and talk to one another and
walk from place to place with important papers, but the
workers on the floor have a sense of humor and for the
most part love that kind of irony, the chance to poke fun
at self-importance. Though they realize how fragile and
dependent those lives are, their dream for their own children is one of those jobs on the other side of that glass.

Several of the workers wear shirts with Cummins
Team Racing logos. It's good, one tells me, to watch the
NASCAR races and see a car with your company name
on it. Like a basketball team in high school, it gives you
something to root for, a team that belongs to you.

Between the glassed-in management and the workers with their NASCAR dreams, you see the future factory: gleaming white like a hospital or an ice palace,

there are no black power-tool wires hanging from the ceiling, no tools for the workers to put their hands around and sense the proper torque and smooth the rough edges. Every few feet there are computers and rows of what appears to be boxy furnaces, every one a taupy white.

The assembly line makes the old N14 engine with its four heads. This is the area gearing up to make the new Signature 600, a gleaming red engine with one head and absolutely no visible parts, a monolith all sexy and powerful. The first engines looked like Singer sewing machines. Not this one. There's nothing pragmatic about it.

In trucking, there are two main customers: the main fleets and then the cowboys—owner operators who aren't particularly good businessmen but who want a macho truck that will look good and have a kick-ass engine. This engine is for boys who want to intimidate the other ones when they lift up their hoods. It's not function that determines the design. It's fashion. The cowboys want an engine with hardly any wires or hoses showing, with all of the mechanism hidden inside the glazed candy-apple red of the machine. It's the same engine—a little smarter due to the computer controlling the timing, for example—it just looks more sleek because, like hospitals and nursing homes and funeral parlors, the real business is hidden under a veneer of glitz. This is an ENGINE.

And it's made in absolute and utter sterility. A futuristic sterility where men in what seem to be lab coats stand in front of computers watching flashing red and green and yellow lights.

You can look hard for an engine here, and you won't see one. The assembly work is done entirely by robots and, like the engine itself, the work is hidden inside those things that look like furnaces. Everything is preset. It's the job of the men and women who run the computers to see when a tool is down to within an inch of its life and to exchange it. That's it. There are small square windows in the furnaces, and you can look inside, but you won't see anything much, I'm told. The job of the human being is to monitor and not to make.

Right now the company makes three or four engines a day, and there are nine people working. When they get up to speed, to eighty or ninety engines a day, they'll hire three more. Twelve people monitoring the production of all the engines and hundreds in the office handling marketing and freight and money. It's a great place to work, one man says as he pokes in numbers on a screen and takes a sip of hot black coffee.

For some reason, maybe because of my age, maybe because I've been thinking about the retirement prospects of the assembly line workers, I look at the rows of metal boxes and I think about all these pesky baby boomers. I think about how worried we are about Social

Security, all the talk about the aging of America. I think about my great-aunt in a health-care center, how much it costs to care for individual bodies as they age, how difficult it is, how families of her generation took care of both the young and of the elderly, how all that's hidden now, like these engines. I think of some creative person with a good idea and of capital trying to increase itself. For some reason I can't walk along this row of hidden robots without thinking of metal tombs, of robot arms handing me my daily medication, checking my vital signs, tucking me into bed at night, filling my head with visions of some Caribbean island or my own child-hood memories so I don't know where I am, hidden away, with no voice to protest that I'm a human being and so is that one hidden in that box beside me and down there and yet again. I think about the workers in Juarez. I wonder where the grandchildren of these few workers will get the money to buy the products that the factories are making, how many of their jobs are built on faith and the work of others. I think about Clessie and Irwin and their eventual falling out.

We're all Clessies now, thinking about a ride that will last a year or two, a good line on the résumé and then a move to the fresher stand of elm. A new century and were heading down the river without caulking seams, without a map. Hoping for the saving grace of genius, luck, or charm.

THE WOMAN WHO SCULPTS
THE DOLLS IS NAMED
VIRGINIA EHRLICH TURNER

Remember thy creator in the days of thy youth.
>   —From the birth certificate of a doll
>   made at the Turner Doll Factory

As in the writing of a novel, there is no real realism;
a landscape, while it may be essentially true to the
scene depicted, always mirrors more or less the content of our consciousness.
>   — T. C. Steele, *The House of the Singing Winds*

It is a little corner that the great strenuous world has
swept around and missed. Whether they are content
with their lot, I do not know.
>   — Selma Steele, as quoted in
>   *The House of the Singing Winds*

Once I had a friend who was in love with dolls. Her
Greenwich Village apartment was filled with them.

When she died, there were only thirteen people at
her funeral, but her grandniece and friends brought her
dolls to the service.

The entire front row was populated with life-sized dolls with mourning faces. And my friend in her casket, all stuffed now with embalming fluid, unmoving and blank as one of the dolls but somehow more so. More so. How can I explain it? The dolls had somehow absorbed her spirit. Not like dolls are always pictured in horror films, not that blank demonic stare that directors give to them. You can look at dolls that way, certainly, but they don't look that way to women, usually. Their faces absorb something from you and reflect it back in ways that mirrors never seem to.

The doll factory isn't easy to find. It doesn't look one bit like a factory. It's three buttercup yellow houses at the top of a hill, surrounded by rolling farmland and trees. They're like the little yellow houses in a Monopoly game.

The town is so small there's no gas station or library to ask directions if you get lost, and my friend Grace and I had to flag down a UPS truck to find our way the final mile.

Up close, you see that the yellow houses are made of sheet metal and are in fact factories in the way that pink Mary Kay Cosmetics cars really are cars. Grace and I park and enter through the retail shop.

Which is filled with extraordinarily beautiful children, almost all of them little girls. They're the kind of dolls you dreamed about when you yourself were a girl, with frilly dresses and pearl buttons that really fasten and soft curls and faces that make you walk from one to another of them and pick them up and hold them close. And there are babies that feel so incredibly real we find ourselves cradling them and cooing and saying, This feels like a real baby, like a real sweet baby, and it's looking at me with upturned eyes, and with such adoration.

Are you looking for anything in particular? The clerk asks us and I say that actually we'd really like to see how these dolls are made.

I'll see if anyone's free, she says, and she disappears into the factory. It takes her so long to return that we think that perhaps these dolls were immaculately conceived, that in fact there is no creator.

I had picked up my friend Grace in Bloomington, and we drove thirty miles through the national forest. The dogwoods were blooming, and you could see last fall's bronze leaves in the deep ravines. The air was warm and the sky cloudless, and Lake Monroe was as blue-green as the Gulf of Mexico. Finally it was spring, and you could feel the gray lift.

This was our second trip in a month's time. Several weeks before we'd driven to the House of the Singing Winds, the former home of the impressionist painter T. C. Steele and his wife, Selma. Now it's a museum. When we were there, Grace was exhausted from the chemo, and she lay on a bench in between viewing paintings. The house was on a high hill, and you could hear the wind sing through the windows. There was a painting of Selma sitting at a desk in the living room and in front of the painting there was a desk and in both the real and fabricated world there was a stuffed peacock with glistening gold feathers.

Today, Grace wore a large straw hat and she had brought a pillow. Everything was green. Even the air was a smoky wash of green, and we drove by pastures filled with horses.

I read Selma's book, I tell Grace. I'd picked up the book in the gift shop the day we went to the museum. I can't seem to go in a gift shop without buying something. My daughter once told me that when she dies, she wants to come back as a mall. Here, she said, and she pointed to her left arm—would be Nordstrom's— and here, she said, pointing to her right—is L. S. Ayres.

It's an amazing book, I said. Selma never once refers to her husband as Ted or T. C. or even Steele, I tell Grace. It's always "the painter."

On her wedding day Steele brought her by rail and then by wagon and then by foot—hours away from the city. Up here in the wilderness. She had dressed herself in French silk crepe with a gray jacket, and she had to walk through miles of mud.

At one point Selma describes Steele taking out a sketchbook and walking away from her. As far as he was concerned, she realized, she no longer existed. It was her wedding day. She was wearing silk crepe in mud as deep as wagon wheels. She tries to talk to him, but he doesn't respond and she thinks at one point about getting back on the train and heading home. She didn't think he would notice. She's angry and crying, and when he turns around he says what a beautiful place this is, how he will come back in better light to paint it.

Right then, I said, she had to decide what she should do.

And she stayed, Grace said.

You're right, I said, she stayed.

She was a painter too, and she made it her job to fully occupy the new house, to break down walls and create the rooms. She even made a vista, cutting down trees in what she visioned as the foreground of a painting. She planted yellow flowers and wisteria vines. She asked the painter how much of his assistance she could count on, and when he said that he really needed all the daylight hours for his own work, she agreed that that seemed plausible.

She was relieved, Grace said.

You're right, I said, she seemed to be. All the rooms in the house were hers, I said, and the land around it, and she built something three-dimensional that wasn't there before. And slowly Selma's creation came into focus for the painter, and she began to see the things that she had made appear on Steele's canvases in her living room.

Vindication, I said.

Or something else, Grace said.

Or something else.

You seem happy, I said. You're doing so well. I'm amazed by you.

Grace looked out the window. The green, she said. You couldn't paint it without it looking false, as though you were applying makeup to the landscape. It was that early green, with more black than yellow.

Grace's hair was silver, with one streak of white, like a halo.

I asked her about the surgery. She'd had good care, an excellent doctor. She talked about the way her breast reacted to the missing tissue.

She leaned her head against the pillow. The chemo made her tired.

At first she'd thought about just having the masectomy, getting rid of the whole thing, she said, and having it reconstructed.

You get a tummy tuck at the same time, she said. Just move it from down there, where you don't want it, to up here.

Do they make a fake nipple or save the old one? I asked. They save the old one, she laughed, and they sew it onto the stomach that's now been molded into a breast shape and sits on your chest.

There's this woman I knew, I told Grace, when I lived in Florida. She'd had breast implants, and when she'd lie down on her back in exercises classes, her breasts wouldn't flatten down, as real breasts do. They'd stay all pointed like a Barbie doll's.

Grace has spent years inside libraries and historical society archives, researching a lost Civil War–era writer named Lilly Blake. Grace has spent her life going through old newspapers to find her stories so she can gather them together. All of Blake's work was out of print when Grace began her work. Now one of the novels is back in print. This woman is a great writer, Grace said. And she'd been erased.

I told her about my great-aunt, who'd been a university teacher in the 1940s.

When the men went to war, all these brilliant women were given jobs in universities. She had been one of the first women admitted to medical school in Indiana, but she'd quit and then gone on to get a master's degree in zoology. She's ninety-eight now and lives in a nursing home. A week ago I finally asked her why she'd dropped out of medical school.

You won't believe this, she told me, I don't think women now could understand it. But I did it for my brother.

Your brother? I asked. Yes, she said. I didn't want him to feel that I had outshone him. He was a smart boy. Our family valued intelligence.

Her brother had taken a job in a factory. She couldn't go on to medical school. He had set the ceiling, and she couldn't rise above it.

But she had come from generations of women who loved science, who were intensely curious.

But the point is, I told Grace on this day as we traveled to the doll factory, that my Aunt May took classes in zoology and before long she had a degree and before long she was teaching at Hunter College in New York. And then she got married and she ended up back here in Indianapolis and then the men went off to war and she began teaching at the local university. And she noticed that the students needed a lab manual, and she wrote the manual so well that her department chairman, as chairmen could do in those days, said it could be a book and he put his name on it along with hers so that it could get published. His name went first. Then he took it to a New York publisher and by the time it was published and then adopted as the leading zoology textbook in the country, which it was for thirty years, it only had his name on it. Her name had been erased from her words.

Was she angry? Grace asked me.

I think she was, I said, though not as much as I would have been. It's something she talks about still. She gave me the evidence—the manual with her name, the intermediate text, and then the final incarnation minus her name. She wants to be remembered for the book. But I think she felt powerless. She felt lucky to have the job she did. There were very few women faculty members.

When the men returned from war, many of the women lost their jobs. There's a clipping in her files about the women faculty members' hobbies. My great-aunt was listed as someone who did needlepoint. One of her friends, a literature professor, wrote a paper about the use of classical mythology on buttons.

When my great-aunt dies, I said, I'm going to fabricate her obituary. I'm going to list her as the author of the book.

You mean, Grace said, you're going to correct a fabrication.

This is the way my conversation went with Grace. As I write it now, it seems dark. But it didn't seem that way when we had this conversation. The sky was blue and the day was warm and gorgeous, and we had a great time, and our time was light. It felt like a holiday.

You seem to be doing so well, I said again, and she said, Yes, though earlier in the winter she'd been terrified.

Then a few weeks ago, she said, she was getting out of the shower. And all of the sudden, she said, the world turned as green as this. She motioned outside the window.

This green, she said. And then she said, You'll laugh, and I said, No, I promise, I won't laugh.

It was just like all the books, she said. I felt this incredible joy, and this was the color the air was, and not a thing was separate from anything and that feeling has never gone away, and it was like every part of my body was made of wires, and all of them were filled with light.

Books are published and then sink like those leaves at the bottom of the ravines we're passing. Next season's leaves fall on top of them, and they're forgotten.

That used to really bother me, Grace said, and now it doesn't quite as much.

A man pours the liquid vinyl into three iron molds of baby heads. The vinyl is pink or chocolate brown or taupe. The molds are capped and put in a furnace that spins the heads in a centrifuge until the vinyl coats the iron mold; then the vinyl is heated so it sticks. When the molds are removed from the furnace, the iron caps have been removed. In iron, the heads look like death masks.

He writes the word *baby* with a Magic Marker on every forehead. Then he takes an ice pick and stabs the back of the sweet pink babies' heads to let out air. He sticks a gloved and oiled hand down into a mold and pops the baby's heated head out into his hand. He holds the baby's head out to us and asks if we want to touch it. The head is so hot it almost burns our fingers. Behind him, on a shelf, there are rows and rows of baby heads and arms and legs. There are boxes marked "Jessica's right arm" or "Samantha's left leg."

The dolls' heads are molded without eyes. Each has a blank, Modigliani-shaped eyespace, but not a space.

There are the eyelids and then an indentation for the football-shaped piece of vinyl that goes behind the eye. So there's something Egyptian about the faces.

There's a hole in the back of the doll's head where the ice pick has gone in, and the man sticks an air hose in through the hole and then fills the head with air. The head blows up like a balloon, like a cartoon head—the cheeks bulging, and the forehead, and finally the indentation where the eye would go, and a woman takes round plastic eyes—the beautifully painted irises surrounded by half-spheres of white, like thick eggs over-easy, and she places them on the bulging eyespaces and then removes the hose. As the air goes out of the head, the eyespaces suck the eyeballs into the head and suddenly the doll gazes adoringly at you.

I know it sounds creepy, but for the most part it's sweet, this process. Women in the town make home-made dresses—the kind with large voile skirts and gorgeous buttons—and molded felt hats with ribbons. And there's a woman who puts a copper mask over each doll's face and paints the lips red by hand and applies blush and eyeshadow. And there's another woman who affixes the eyelashes and trims the lower ones, and a woman who dresses the dolls, and a woman who applies the wigs over the holes in their heads using a glue gun. And there's a woman who stuffs the torsos with cotton and who ties the heads to the bodies and the arms and legs and who puts the final stitch in the back of the torso and who numbers each doll's neck with ink: No. 1 out of 200, No. 45 out of 2,000. Each doll is made from a handmade sculpture, each one a limited edition, each one gorgeous. There's a woman whose job it is to brush each doll's beautiful hair before placing it in a box and another woman whose job it is to prepare them for shipping, and they all take turns naming the dolls and coming up with their stories.

Don't tell my husband how much it cost, Grace says, and I say, Are you kidding? I didn't grow up watching those episodes of *I Love Lucy* for nothing. You always cut the price by half or hide the purchase in a closet until you can pull it out with a "this old thing?" Of course.

There's a man on a cigarette break outside the factory when we leave the place. He laughs at the way we're holding our new babies. You must see this all the time, we say to him. Of course, he says.

And he explains how he bought one last Christmas for his mother, and that strikes both Grace and me as infinitely sweet and wonderful. You'd better buckle them in your car, he said, because when I was bringing that doll home I was stopped by the police. He thought I was carrying a child without a child restraint. He laughs. I had to tap the doll's face, he said, to prove it wasn't real.

The poet Rilke was terrified of dolls. He saw, in their blank and unresponding faces, both God's silence and the silence of the dead. No matter how steadfast your prayer, he thought, a doll will never acknowledge your existence.

How could anyone so smart about angels have been so absolutely wrong about dolls. Or maybe it's one of those paradoxes. You can only see the doll's spirit if you believe in it. Oh well. It's Rilke's loss.

All I know is that Grace and I stared at those babies' faces as though they were real, and they were. For Rilke, the doll's face was fixed and unresponsive. For Grace and me, the face responded infinitely. How in the world can I explain the way it seems to move? I know it's my own eye that moves, from the doll's mouth to its eyes to its mouth again. But it's the doll's face that seems to strobe with life. Each arc of the strobe is like a heart-beat, a pulse; only, instead of light or blood, the rhythm measures something more mysterious. Nothing exists outside that face, not even Rilke.

The dolls we'd picked were dressed in blue, in-tended to be boys. Mine had a tag that said its name was Samuel. But we dismissed that blue. These were our daughters' faces. No doll is ever a boy, not really. We cradled the vinyl babies in our arms. We cooed as we looked down at them. How beautiful yours is, we said, waiting for the return compliment. We buckled them into the car seatbelt. Grace's husband would laugh as we drove up to her house. He told us we'd lose our rank if they saw us at the university. What had gotten into us? Some madness, we said, some spring madness.

When you see a row of dolls' heads, even when they have different expressions, as these do, you realize that dolls are always made to look up at you. Dolls in horror films stare straight out, but dolls that girls will love look up with trust, and you want to protect them. Adults are taller, obviously, than little girls, but most men will be taller as well. It's the gaze that women are used to giving but only receive in their adult lives from their children, and then only temporarily.

We called the babies "she." Our own fragile souls look up at us with wonder from the backseat of the car, some universal female spirit we were gazing at in admiration. We would keep the spirit alive. We would tell them stories. How beautiful yours is, Grace says to me. And yours, I say to her, and yours.

PERFECT CIRCLE

A WORLD IN MOTION BEGINS WITH YOU!
—Advertising copy, TEDCO Industries

Goodbye to Raintree Co., incorrigible enthusiast of
ideas. Goodbye to the good small roads of Raintree
County, the horse and buggy roads. Hard roads and
wide will run through Raintree County and its ancient boundaries will dissolve. People will hunt it on
the map, and it won't be there.
—Ross Lockridge, *Raintree County*

Part One

It's Janus's month, and I know I should be trying to see
in two directions. But the ground is covered with ice and
snow and I feel as though I'm spinning on one of those
thin rings of time that occur at the turn of a century.

Though there is no simple spinning. The blood is
made of iron from some spinning distant supernova; it

spins around the heart in elliptical circles like the earth around the sun. The bodies of each star and planet spin. *Walk to the well,* Rumi wrote. *Turn as the earth and the moon turn, circling what they love. Whatever circles comes from the center.*

Yesterday a friend demonstrated the dance of the dervishes to me in the middle of a swirling snowstorm. I wanted to know what a dervish did. My friend is not a dervish, but he knows things.

Like this, he said, his hand in the air, the one foot working like a turning pump. The dresses are so heavy they take on the power of gravity, he said. It's centrifugal force, like a gyroscope.

Or like a centrifuge, he said, it distills until you're down to essence.

It's the dresses that fling the dancers in the circles finally, and it's the earth that keeps them going, the dresses working like a machine, an engine, inducing a kind of drunkenness in the dancers.

It's a drunkenness, Sufi poet Rumi wrote, that brings you closer to the circling of the earth and moon and to love: the "secret turning in us" that "makes the universe turn." The earth spins, the stars spin, lovers spin in secret and confusion.

There's a thing called gyrodivination, where you spin in a circle and fall down onto prophecy. Onto prophecy, which is a place. Shakers spinning in Kentucky, longing for God. Spun candy, spun threads, spinning fiberglass, the hair of an angel.

Yesterday, wherever I drove in my life, I looked at the wheels on cars and not the box. The wheels spin in circles, and the box moves in a line.

The spinning stops at certain lights and then begins again. When it stops, you can see the individual spokes, and when it starts, all you see is glittering silver. We spin, in our gasoline-powered cars, around the city.

It was Epiphany Sunday, star Sunday, the final tightest spin of the retreating millennium. The tighter and smoother the ring inside the piston, the more perfect the circle, the stronger the combustion.

I'm writing this essay in an abandoned car factory, the day after the last Epiphany Sunday of the millennium. I don't know exactly what was made in the particular space where I'm working. Someone made some part of a car. I don't know what part. What I do in this office now is sit on a chair and type on a keyboard and look out a transom-style window onto an asphalt roof and into another artist's window. That's the only vision from this window, so I work in here until I've used up all the fuel and then I go outside to bring in more.

The woman who rents the office next to mine comes in every once in a while in a whirl of energy. She paints. Sometimes she accidentally locks herself in her office, and she has to call maintenance on her cell phone. The man on the other side does paperwork for a micro-brewery and listens to Rush Limbaugh on the radio. Across the hall, next to the Coke machine, there's a sculptor who works with large objects and plays loud music while he works, and then a photography studio, and then a massage therapist whose office smells like lavender.

There are still car-sized elevators at the end of the hall, and the building is always clean and smells of PineSol mixed with the lavender. The building is still called the Stutz, and the man who owns the building now collects burnished cars and keeps them scattered on the loading dock in odd open spaces in between the artist studios and balloon companies and massage therapists and computer repair offices and detective agencies. When I come here in the morning I pass a giant Texaco pump in the lobby and sometimes at lunch there will be an odd-looking vintage raspberry-colored gangster car out on the sidewalk, with running boards and high slotted windows.

The last Stutz Bearcat was made here in the late 1930s. The first one was made in 1911 for the inaugural Indianapolis 500-mile race. A whirling that takes place outside the winds of prophecy, the race is more like some whirling both created from and in opposition to the winds of death. Though maybe there is no real difference.

I can picture men building where I'm working now. Let's put on one god-damn helluva show, the boss says.

They were boys really, with a life expectancy not much more than fifty. They were young with the century, they would live forever; they believed the past was dead, and that time would always be unfolding, a double helix, a relaxing spring.

Many of them would be drafted and fight or design engines in the century's wars, but they couldn't imagine it, not then. Or maybe they could. Maybe at some level it was inevitable and had something to do with boys and machinery and a love for speed. At any rate, they made a car that would race around the track with cars built by other boys—Duesenberg, Cummins, Marmon, Packard, Studebaker. You'd recognize the names.

The first Stutz was conceived and designed and built by hand in, they say, five weeks just so it could compete in the first 500. The band that played for that first race was the Perfect Circle Band.

Sometimes time slows down, a wobbling wheel; we're almost drugged and waiting to awaken. The monk Mendel published his papers on genetics sixteen years before other scientists were ready to discover what they meant. It was of course in 1900 that we were prepared to understand them. Everything happened around 1900. Just think of the books that were published: *Sister Carrie, Jude the Obscure, The Awakening, The Cherry Orchard.* One word those texts have in common is *awakening.* The word our own texts have in common is *numbness.*

Still. Imagine knowing one secret to the universe for sixteen years and watching everyone else bumbling around you. You wonder what we're asleep to now. You shake yourself. Wake up. Whatever it is, it's already there if we could only see it.

Sometimes time itself seems to become a dervish, a loop that seems to spin with its own internal force.

In 1893, Mr. Ferris's giant light-covered wheel soared 264 feet high above the Chicago World's Fair, burning its perfect circle into the imagination, and by the early 1900s there were more successful automobile companies in Indianapolis, Indiana, just hours south, than any place else in the world.

And at the other edge of this same century, I sit here typing words in a machine that could not have been imagined one hundred years ago, while a surviving Stutz Bearcat dreams its eternal flapper dreams in the basement of this building and Captain Balloon fills a room with temporary helium-filled mylar for someone's party. I've lived my entire life, almost half a century, in this circle city. Much of that life I've spent inside a car.

The man who perfected piston rings and invented cruise control lived his life in Hagerstown, Indiana—one hour east of here by car. He made the piston rings for the Stutz Bearcat. The name of his company was

Perfect Circle. Maybe the office where I'm sitting is where the shaft and pistons were assembled. I like to think so.

The man's name was Ralph Teetor. He was a perfectionist and for a while built handmade engines that were too good for the cars they were placed into. When he invented cruise control, he built it so carefully that it was more well made, again, than the cars themselves. So the large companies learned how to make them. Long story.

He began, as did all the boys who worked on planes and cars, by building bicycles. His first invention was a bicycle carriage that went on railroad tracks and that was used to inspect the rails. He built a company to manufacture them, and then he made a car and then he specialized in rings. Piston rings look like one cut-off spiral from a Slinky toy.

He was a brilliant engineer, and his brain, it seemed, was also combustible. To read about his life is to read about the life of any creative human being. It's fitting that there are artists in the building where the carboys created their machines. Teetor was an artist. When he woke up each day he had ideas, he had ideas all day long, and he put them into practice. He invented special doors for his house, he invented a suitcase to more efficiently pack his clothes. He designed a way to take the kink out of a creek, and he built a levee in Hagerstown that wasn't needed until a one-hundred-year flood fifty-six years later, long after he was gone, and when the flood came, the levee worked perfectly. He made all those piston rings for the cars at the early 500 races. He was one of those boys who traveled around in the combustion of midwestern carboys at the beginning of the twentieth century.

And from the age of seven, Ralph Teetor was completely, absolutely blind. In 1893 he saw the ferris wheel and in 1896 they removed the ball of his eye. The other eye turned dark in sympathy. He never forgot the wheel.

So much can happen in a few years. In 1908 Hagerstown was wired for electric lights. The power was on from sundown until 11:00 p.m. Soon Tuesday morning, laundry day, was added so women could push their electric irons in circles on their husbands' shirts.

For years, Teetor's workshop was in the basement of his house. It was filled with engines and lathes, machinery that could cut your finger off if you weren't careful, and because he was blind he had no need for lights. Imagine it. Your husband, say, or your son or father, in a basement workshop seething with motors, all of them experimental, the awful sounds, and the hands with no eyes to guide them, that delicate skin a hair's breadth from a spinning lathe or sharp blade, from a belt that could slip, from the grinding insensitivity of a machine. Imagine too the opposite: hands that are so finely tuned they can sense an object and where it is and what it's made of before the hands actually touch it.

It's winter. I close my eyes and move my hands slowly toward a window. I concentrate on the sense of touch. It doesn't take much practice until I can feel the increasing coldness as my fingertips near the glass and I know the precise moment when I'll feel it on my skin.

I try it with the bookshelf. It's more difficult. The air about an eighth of an inch from the veneer is slightly cooler than the air a quarter-inch away, but still the moment when my hand touches the bookshelf comes as a surprise. Now, now, now—and thud, misjudged again. Although in theory the universe may be made of dots with nothing in between them and although it may be all of one thing, in practice you need to know the boundaries, the edge between one thing and another. In theory, it would be great if the universe worked like shuffling cards—your hand made of planes, the bookcase made of planes, and when they come in contact the cards stack, and it's all one thing. If the Sufis and Shakers can spin themselves in perfect circles and come down feeling like one stack of shuffled cards, more power to them, they'll still stub their toes on the corner of that sofa, though I suppose at that point it won't matter.

But I work and work at trying to anticipate an object with my hand. A chair, a picture frame, a bed. There's a tension you have to get beyond, but then you feel it. It has to do with temperature and a tingling of the skin. You feel an object in space, but it's painful to hold yourself that still for long. You want to give up trying. You want to just let go. You would, if you were blind, perhaps, become obsessed with circles. You start in one place and know it's in the nature of a circle to bring you back where you began.

Ralph would snap his fingers to listen for the echo to locate things in space. At any rate, it's possible, but not easy, to see the world half darkly through your fingertips. I can't imagine doing it with any speed, and speed's the thing for carboys. I can't imagine the courage it would take to decide to follow the muse when it led you to engineering, and you had no eyes.

The outline of an engine was clearer to Teetor than the outline of his own face. Until Schick came out with electric razors, he went to the barbershop every day for a shave so he wouldn't nick his lip or nose.

When he began to manufacture rings on an assembly line, his company, Perfect Circle, was the biggest employer in Hagerstown. Children who lived along the route he walked to work learned to keep toys off the sidewalk. You didn't want to be the child who caused Mr. Teetor to fall and your father to lose his job.

Still, he was so good at navigating that you could know him for a week, it was said, and not figure out that he was blind until someone left a door ajar that wasn't meant to be ajar and Teetor, thinking with such intensity about his workshop, say, temporarily lost his batlike sense of objects in space and ran into the door. His face was often covered with knots and bruises.

He had to talk his way into engineering school and they wouldn't let him graduate without passing an exam with graphs. So he built a graph of nails and string and did his graphing three-dimensionally.

It's said that when John Muir was in the Rocky Mountains, he often lived on bread and coffee. It's said that he could fall down cliffs without breaking a bone. He rolled himself into a ball and whirled down the mountain like a tumbleweed.

Epiphany Sunday afternoon my son went spinning down a frozen hill on a plastic saucer. He went spinning at the same time I asked my friend to demonstrate the dance of the dervishes to me.

Like this, he said. Like this.

When I told my friend my son was sledding, my friend told a story about the day he and five of his friends decided it would be a good idea to take their sleds to the top of a hill and start down at once, all heading for the same distant point. Why? I asked. He said they all decided it would be exciting.

Was it? I asked, and he said that yes it was, it was amazing. All five of them came together in an amazing clash of sleds and bodies, an explosion of boys and wood and metal. It was, he said, the only time he's ever been inside a thing like that, that it was like being inside a process, inside combustion. There were a lot of injuries though, he said—broken legs and arms—and surgeries.

In one second it went from thrilling to a groaning battlefield. But that one moment, he said, that one moment really was amazing.

Teetor was an engineer. He was brilliant. He was probably in many ways rigid. He had to be. When he built his house, he could sense when a floor or step wasn't level, and he had the floor or step rebuilt. Remember, he took the kink out of a creek. In order to keep from falling, he had to be alert and those around him had to keep things in a certain order.

He was a brilliant man and a good father and husband, and he felt that he was doing something good for the place he lived. "The first investment of capital in a few machines," he said, "created jobs for just a few men.

"Then as more and more capital was added to the business, more machines and men were needed."

Jobs outside the home created lives for families, lives that then depended on the jobs, the shopkeepers, the truckers bringing food from distant farms. His business went from simple cottage industry to manufactory to a factory employing close to 2,000 people, all beginning to grow dependent, in ways they were afraid to acknowledge, on technology and corporations far beyond their control.

He was a good father. You give your children life, he must have thought. You don't understand when they claim those lives for themselves. You don't understand when they disobey you. Surely they will always love you.

Surely they will understand your sacrifices. Surely they won't begrudge you the fine house, the lovely cars, the perfect family. Surely they will know that you are the central character in this drama, that their lives depend on you. How could they not know this story? How could they ever be so blind?

In 1955, years after the bitter labor disputes of the 1930s, an old-style labor war broke out at Perfect Circle. I remember living in that county in the early 1980s and listening to old women talk about the strike days, how their husbands or fathers made them keep guns next to them in the front seat of their cars. I didn't pay much attention at the time to those women and their stories, and most of them are gone now, so I have to go back to newspapers and magazines to reconstruct the story.

At the time, if I was interested in anything they said, it was the things that sounded like myth. I remember their stories about roses with buds the size of your fist and stems that reached clear to the ground. I remember the roses were some hybrid created at a German greenhouse in New Castle, that no one knew the way back to those particular roses now. I remember they were used to decorate the ceiling of the Waldorf Astoria in New York when prince something-or-other visited from England.

I remember learning how bees made honey. I remember a woman whose grandmother was in a tug of war with a tornado—a tornado that made the jog on

Walnut Street—because it threatened to pull her good silk dress out a second-story window. She pulled the dress back in, and she wore it to a dance.

I remember the Victorian hair wreaths at the Historical Society Museum. I remember the women talking about special dress fabrics ordered from overseas, fabrics handmade and threaded with gold or silver, so beautiful you couldn't imagine. I remember an ancient woman saying that in her girlhood you could buy an abortion for the price of one good ruby.

I was a girl, and I paid attention to the stories about being girls. I couldn't care less about strikes or factories. I couldn't get my mind around the perfect circle of the barrel of a gun.

The national journalists who covered the strike were amazed by it, and in retrospect it still seems inexplicable. The times were good and there was almost a mutual assured destruction pact between unions and managements. They were more equal in power than at other times. Contracts were negotiated. It was right after the war, and no one wanted violence. It was Mr. Teetor's company, he was committed to the place, he knew the employees, he was blind, How could it happen to him? What kind of world was this becoming?

Old-Style Labor War exploded in Indiana. Bitter 10-week strike produces bloody gunfight as union tries to shut down an embittered foundry. The article in the *Nation* was titled "Perfect Circle—Back to Bayonets."

None of the journalists could understand it. It was out of time, out of history. There was nothing at stake other than stubbornness. The salaries were good, the company had offered a new benefits package, a raise. The UAW wanted a union shop, a guarantee that an employee who didn't pay his dues would lose his job. Mr. Teetor wanted the employees to choose. Some of the employees came down on the side of the union. Some of them came down on the side of the company. But it wasn't a crisis, not something that needed to be decided in a day. And still, violence broke out and escalated.

The strike lasted twelve days. During that time, nonstrikers fired guns from the factory; strikers fired guns from outside. They attempted to break down iron gates. The lieutenant governor called in the police. The governor called in the national guard and declared martial law. There were thousands of demonstrators, eight wounded; there were World War II M-17s and, as Walter Fall wrote in the *Nation,* "People blamed both the company and the union and watched dejectedly as fresh-faced youngsters of the Indiana National Guard cruised the streets in jeeps, bayonets fixed." They were boys, they were sliding down a hill toward one point, and there was an explosion. In the middle of it all a group of strikers recognized blind stubborn Teetor and his wife on a street corner in his hometown and he spun in circles with his cane raised, trying to explain himself.

Part Two

A month ago I drove to Hagerstown, looking for the Perfect Circle company. While the Stutz building houses artists and not assembly lines, I knew that the Teetor Development Corporation still remained in some form. Teetor Engineering Development Company was listed in the phone book. And it was a beautiful day for a drive, the sky a cat's eye marble blue.

I've always loved Hagerstown. When we were in our twenties, my husband and I used to drive there on Friday nights for dinner and too much bourbon, and we'd walk around the town where Teetor walked and point out front porches we'd like to sit on, antique stores where we'd buy our plates and furniture, houses where we'd live with Oriental rugs and a wood-burning fireplace and candy-colored stained-glass lamps. We'd walk into town and buy homemade donuts on Saturday morning at the donut shop and homemade caramels at the candy shop, and the children we'd someday have would ride their glittering bicycles through the golden angel dust that lined the street and we would know the names of the women who worked at the hardware store and the pharmacist with his bottles filled with blue- and yellow-tinctured water and we would always every minute of our lives be happy.

I drove into town a month ago and wasn't disappointed. The day was perfect, the candy store was still where it had always been, and the restaurant where we ate dinner, and the antique stores. I parked by the lot where the tent theater was set up every summer and remembered sitting in the heat with friends and buying popcorn and watching college students perform *Brigadoon* with the circle of canvas above our heads. Like Brigadoon, now, Hagerstown sleeps Monday through Wednesday and opens Thursday through the weekend. It was Monday, but I found a place open for lunch— through a gate into the first floor of a Victorian house. There were Reubens and grilled cheese and club sandwiches, a table full of CDs and tapes being organized, and another table full of what seemed like ribbons and pine cones and glitter for making wreaths. You could see back into the kitchen where the cook was working, and she seemed like your mom, and the bookstore was closed while the bookstore owner ate lunch at the table next to the one where I was sitting, and when I eavesdropped I heard old friends from two different churches talking about how to attract teenagers to their services. It was all just as I remembered it.

After lunch, I walked down Washington Street toward Factory Boulevard, the site of Perfect Circle for one hundred years. Along the route were small arts-and-crafts-style workers houses—nothing fancy or ostentatious, perfectly groomed—no gutters hanging askew, no peeling paint, no clutter. It was that kind of day, that kind of place—like a town created by an artisan with a vision, a sense of harmony and history, a town built originally around mills with their grinding wheels and then around a perfect silver ring.

I thought of words I associate with my grandmother, words I never hear used—frugality and thrift, economy. Greed is one of the seven deadly sins for a good reason. Treat everything as though it has a soul. I love having these kinds of thoughts. I feel cleansed. I feel good. We'll live in one of those tiny houses with just a few things and each thing will have its own cupboard (that old-fashioned word!) built into the wall and I'll play the violin and my daughter the piano and my son the bass and my husband the cello and we won't have a single television and once a week we'll putt along in a slow-moving vintage car to one of those churches where they're trying to recruit teenagers and it will feel as though the earth is a river and we're floating on it.

I get to the end of the street and there, at the corner of Washington and Factory, is the Perfect Circle building, just where it's always been. A company so committed to a place that the street is named Factory. Here's the factory, the street is Factory. Here's the church, the street is Church. Here's Schoolhouse Lane and Susan Drive and (your name) Boulevard. The universe is understandable. You can walk from one place to another even if you're blind. Everything has its place and will always be right where you left it last. No more lost keys or glasses in the early morning. The factory is a blue-green parallelogram. I could have found it in the dark.

Of course there's a *For Sale* sign on the Perfect Circle building.

No. Impossible. Some cynical part of my brain has created this hallucination, some part of the brain that loves irony. This business was made here, it was thought of here, it's as connected to the history of this place as a heart. Even though that history has that violent side, it gives its story depth, is part of the fall from grace of any human system, part of the recognition that it is in fact a *human* system. Like our government, like a cradle, it will always hold us.

Which means, I suppose, that it's impermanent, and I'm simply once again mourning that impermanence.

In a field next to the abandoned building there's a marker. A circle with an ellipses and a PC in the center. In 1905, the sign says, the Light Inspection Car Company, Teetor's bicycle railway company, began producing engines for American Auto Company in Indianapolis. In 1914 it became the Teetor-Harley Motor Company. It supplied handmade engines for Auburn, American, Stutz, Marmon, Peerless. In 1918 it sold the engine business and concentrated on piston rings, ending, the sign says "the jack-of-all-trades era" and entering "the age of industrial specialization."

For years, the company was owned and run by members of the family. Eventually they were bought out, and exactly one hundred years after the whole thing began, the new company moved operations out of Hagerstown. All that's left here now is this sign.

On the southeast corner of Washington and Factory is the abandoned building. On the southwest corner is a field bounded by the railroad track and the sign. On the northeast corner the houses begin. But on the northwest corner!

It's TEDCO, Teetor's one-story building where, as the business grew, he and his engineers invented things. It was built for Perfect Circle in the 1940s as a testing facility for piston rings. At one time, I knew, there was an undergound tunnel connecting the thinking building to the making one across the street. It wasn't where the suits who make more money thinking about making more money worked; it was the place for quirky mathematicians and engineers, the creative types. Some of the machinery designed in that place was so beautiful you wouldn't mind having it in your living room as a sculpture. During the 1940s there were men crisscrossing underneath the street corner where I'm standing. Something remains: perhaps the essence of it all. Perhaps it's been distilled to the simple joy of it.

The inside of the building is painted a pale gray-blue. It's light and cheerful like a grade school. You can see into the employee lunchroom down the hall, and there are large windows and bright red flowers on the table like the kind of flowers a magician would pull from his jacket sleeve. In the lobby there's a life size poster of

Bill Nye, the science guy from PBS. *Hey hey!* says the balloon coming from his mouth. *This is way-cool Science! Check out the science of spin!*

The Perfect Circle has spun and spun and spun until it came down in the valley of love and delight. Simple gifts. The man who shows me around the building is an elf.

They manufacture toys.

They don't sell to the large discount places. They don't try to compete with Mattel or Hasbro, companies that manufacture toys in the Orient and sell them in bulk, and cheaply, those toys not meant to last for much longer than the initial rush, those toys you never think of handing down to your grandchildren.

But these TEDCO toys are the kind that Santa's elves make in movies. They're the kind of toys that teach you something, they're fascination and simple wonder, the kinds of elemental toys that you simply stare at: blocks and marbles with 209, 715, 200, 000, 000, 000, 000, 000, 000 combinations. Laser discs that are cardboard printed with holographic paper. You watch them spin on a table. Prisms that you watch the day through. Magna Tricks, which are orange, blue, and yellow magnetized lifesavers on a pedestal. You push on them and if they're stacked just right, they repel one another and fly up in the air.

But they specialize in gyroscopes that are sold in mom-and-pop toy stores and in specialty and museum shops. You buy a gyroscope in the Smithsonian, and it will say Smithsonian on the box, but it was manufactured here. Ditto for the gyros you buy at the Henry Ford Museum, the California Science Center, the Museum Company, the Museum of Science and Industry in Chicago, the Denver Museum of Science and Nature, the Ontario Science Center, the Oregon Museum of Science and Industry. Some of their gyroscopes were taken up in the space shuttle.

This place is the epicenter of spin.

It's a cottage industry, a clean, well-lighted pastel place. It takes six people to fabricate a gyroscope. They sit at tables or beautifully crafted machines. Sparks fly from two of the machines—those cool sparks like the ones that come out of sparklers on July 4th. It makes the place seem festive.

Bars of metal are melted at 800 degrees and put in molds. What kind of metal? It's linotype. No, I say. Yes, they answer. It's the linotype from old printing presses—fifty-five-gallon drums of letters, language, old books melted down to their joyful essence, the way language spins you up out of yourself like the spume of a whale. In this place, letters are molded into a spinning wheel, a kind of poetry. A woman named Cheryl breaks off the sprue—what letters? unnecessary repetition, an extra *and* or *the*? She knocks it off and perfects the wheel. That's her job, and the sprues are melted back down and the process begins again, and the whole process sounds like staples.

There's a woman who puts the gyro wheels on a turner, then grabs a brush and dips it in a Cheez Whiz or pickle jar. The wheel spins in front of her, and she paints them with that see-through primary glossy stuff that went on popcorn bowls in the fifties. I tell her I think I'd like her job, watching the wheel spin and holding the brush at just the right angle to get the color even. If you get the paint and brushes just right, she said, it's not a bad job. You have to like crafts.

I could watch the spin all day, I tell her. She tells me I might think I'd like to, but it would make me sick.

In the final step they put the wheel and frame together. The spot welding machine is the one that makes the sparks. There are tiny ball bearings that go inside to make them work. A gyroscope is simpler than a car engine and more elemental. It will keep its balance no matter where you start it spinning, and it will always always keep its relation to the spinning earth.

There are simple gyroscopes and then the gravitron, a gyroscope in a plastic space ship–like thing for nineties kids. It has a purple frame, a green wheel, a clear case.

Travis, my guide, started one of the gravitrons spinning, and he handed it to me to hold. Hold a gyroscope in your hand, and it takes over your arm. You try to move it off balance, and it pulls itself back. It's a powerfully quirky thing.

It's noisy in injection molding where they make pedestals for the gyros in primary colors. They're running bright yellow now. Red is the most expensive plastic to run. Red is $36 a pound. Black is $5. Yellow is $10. Yellow is the color of the Bill Nye pedestal, of my true love's hair.

The plastic is 100 percent recycled. They mix the plastic sprue and color in an old cement mixer. Travis's brother Thurnia ("That's my Dad's name too") runs every machine in this building. He mixes virgin and regrind plastic—enough new plastic to keep getting a clear box, so you can see the gyros. The pellets fill a huge barrel. You can tell the virgin pellets because they're extruded plastic, like gerbil food.

This is where they make the prisms. They come in huge fifty-pound sheets of acrylic all covered with a haze. The haze you see, Thurnia tells me, is actually scratches. The key to making prisms is to remove the haze, like polishing precious stones.

A TEDCO toy has to be educational, has to be high quality, has to be fun. *Imagination has no bounds* is their slogan. You can walk through doors, you can see around corners. You can stay in one place and drive to the moon.

Perhaps, like a crust of bread or a rind of fruit, this ring of time will seem like something at the edge of sweetness, the leftover, or the thing that held the freshness in. Or perhaps it will seem like a piston ring that held back the past and allowed the kind of combustion that creates an explosive future, a future we can't clearly imagine but are already giving birth to.

Outside my factory window the snow is whirling and inside the Washington beltway the politicians are arguing over whether to impeach a president. For an entire year, the television airwaves have been filled with men and women trying to finally crack open the mystery of who the president is. Like a poem or a prism, there's the surface and the infinite number of ways it can be read or turned to capture light. Fascination. Who is he? Who are we if everything is in fact a fabricated fiction? We spin around the object of fascination, and it feels vertiginous. When you feel dizzy, you try to stop yourself from spinning or you give into it. It seems as though you're one type of person or the other. You take a stand. Or perhaps, the problem is, you're both.

Duplicity and change. Robert Louis Stevenson wrote *Dr. Jekyll and Mr. Hyde* near the turn of the last century. Dostoyevsky wrote *The Double.* Chekhov wrote "Lady with the Dog" and *The Cherry Orchard.* Kate Chopin wrote *The Awakening.* Theodore Dreiser wrote *Sister Carrie* and Thomas Hardy wrote *Jude the Obscure.* At the turn of the century we feel the new world being born inside of us, and we're somehow ashamed and frightened of it. We look back with nostalgia at the past. But our century was not one century, but two. It split right down the center with the atom. It splits right through the Perfect Circle, and the first half ended with Ralph Teetor spinning blindly with his cane on a street corner. We look toward the future with joy and then with horror. What have we done? What have we made here? Where are we going?

In the basement of TEDCO, the tunnel that goes across to the factory is boarded off. You can't go there. But the people who work at the toy company like to come down here and think about the 1940s when Perfect Circle was in its prime and seemed as though it would last forever. The basement is painted yellow, but it's more of a borderland between the factory and the playscape. Still, it's pleasant, and interesting that a company formed by someone who was blind should be so visually pleasing. Maybe, if you're blind, you are in fact more aware of the light coming through the windows, that there's something about a pleasant space that has nothing to do with visual aesthetics, is even deeper than that, more multileveled an experience, that the beauty is in fact the outward and visible sign of a more perfect form. What I'm saying is that even the basement is comforting.

In the back there's an old photo lab and signs left from the 1940s. *Emergency Fire Shower. Photographic Department Research.*

And in the center of the basement there's a storage area, and the storage area is filled with antique toys: Wheelos. Pig Mania. Yo-yos. Board games and dolls in their original boxes.

It's for inspiration, Travis says. We come down here when we want to remember how it feels to be a kid. We come down here, he says, to remember things that last.